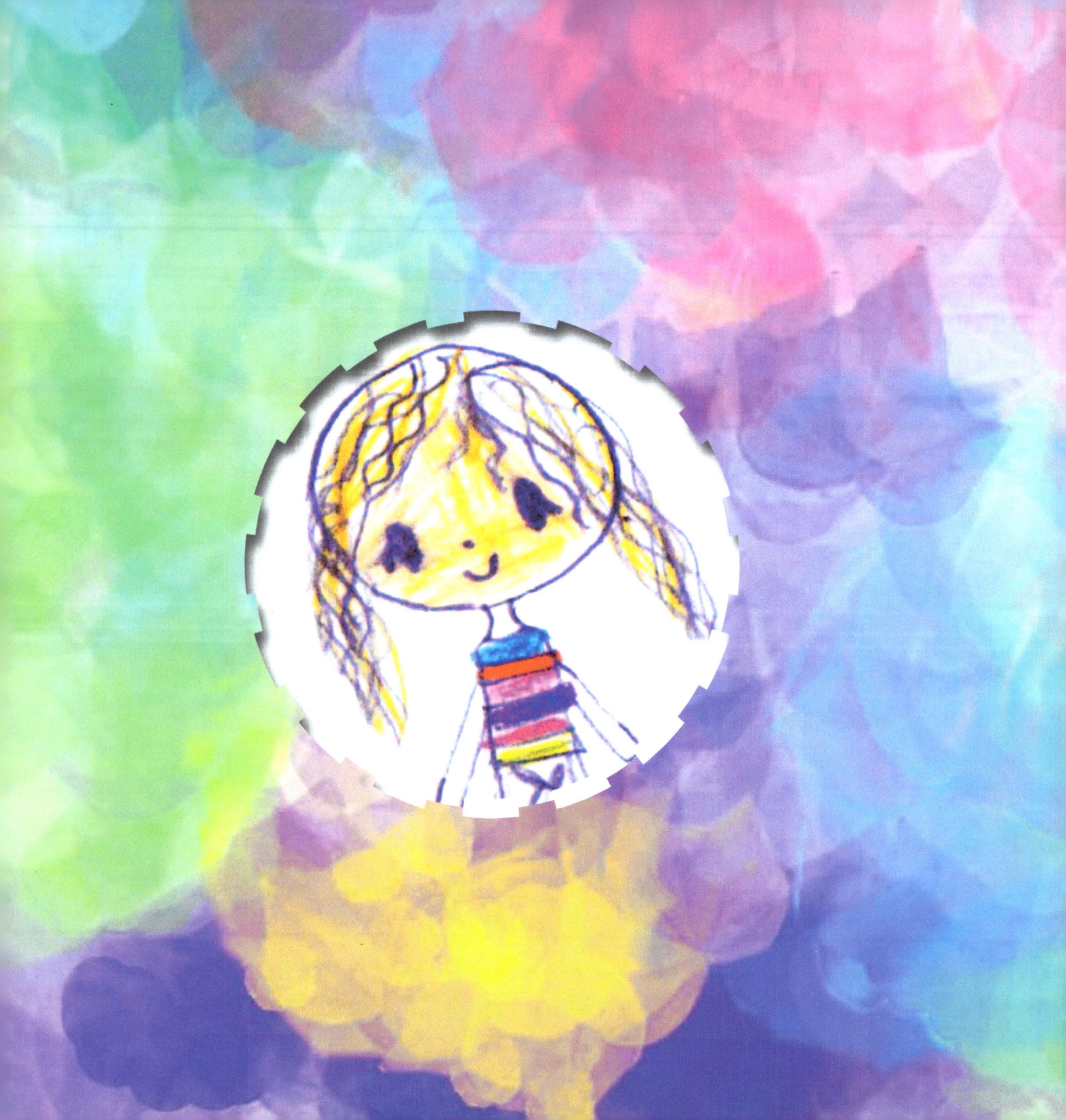

Hi my name is Liv
and I am 7 years old.

I love drawing and painting.
Here I tell the story about my
last drawings.

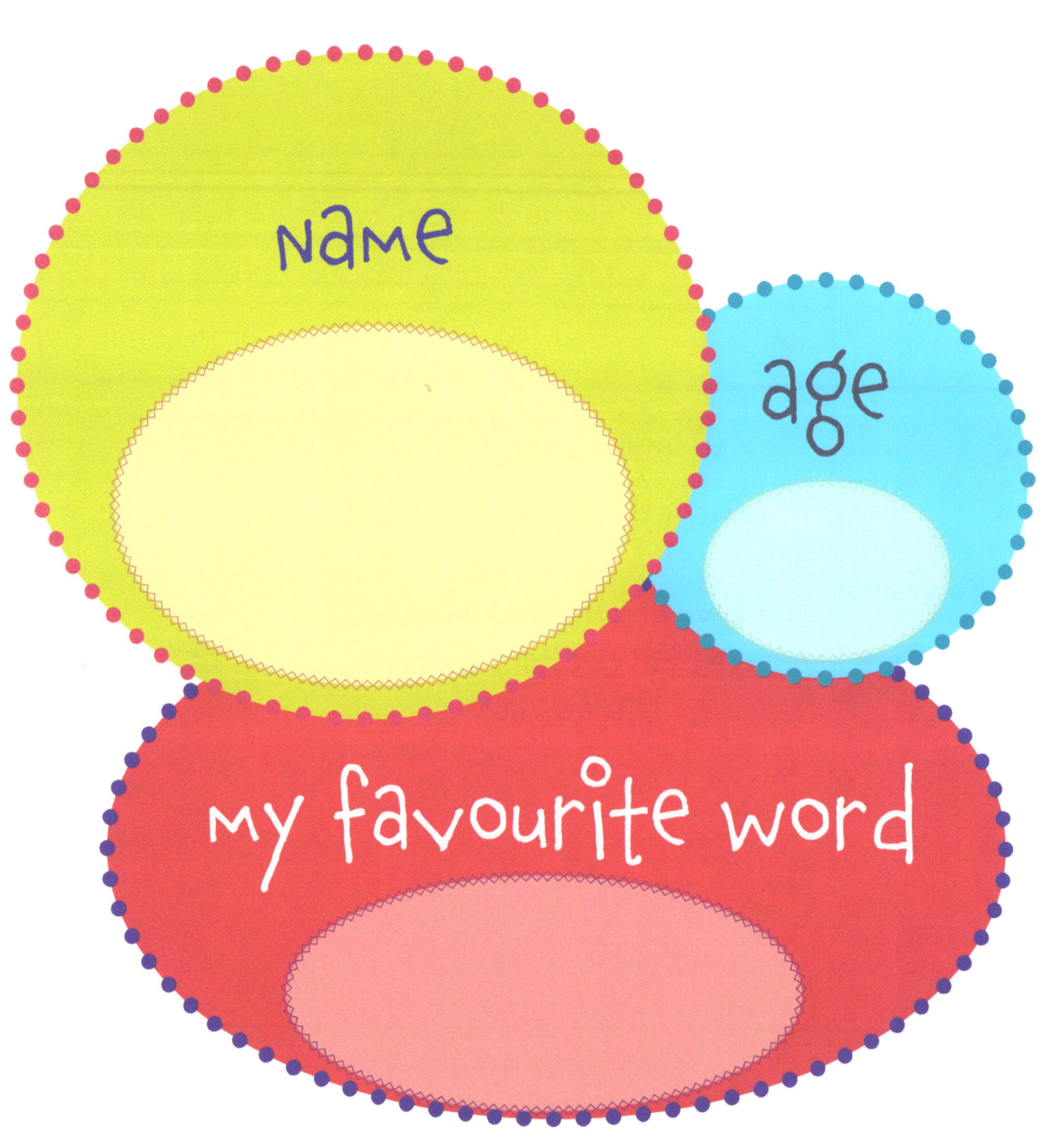

   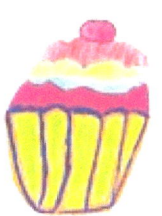 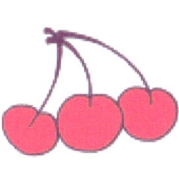 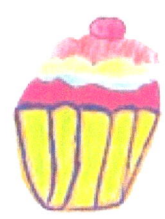

TO 'MUMY' AND 'DADY'

I like the way you take care of me and hug me.

LIV

 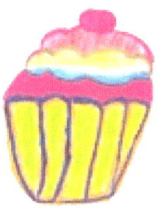 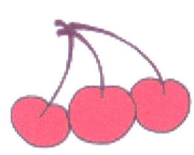   

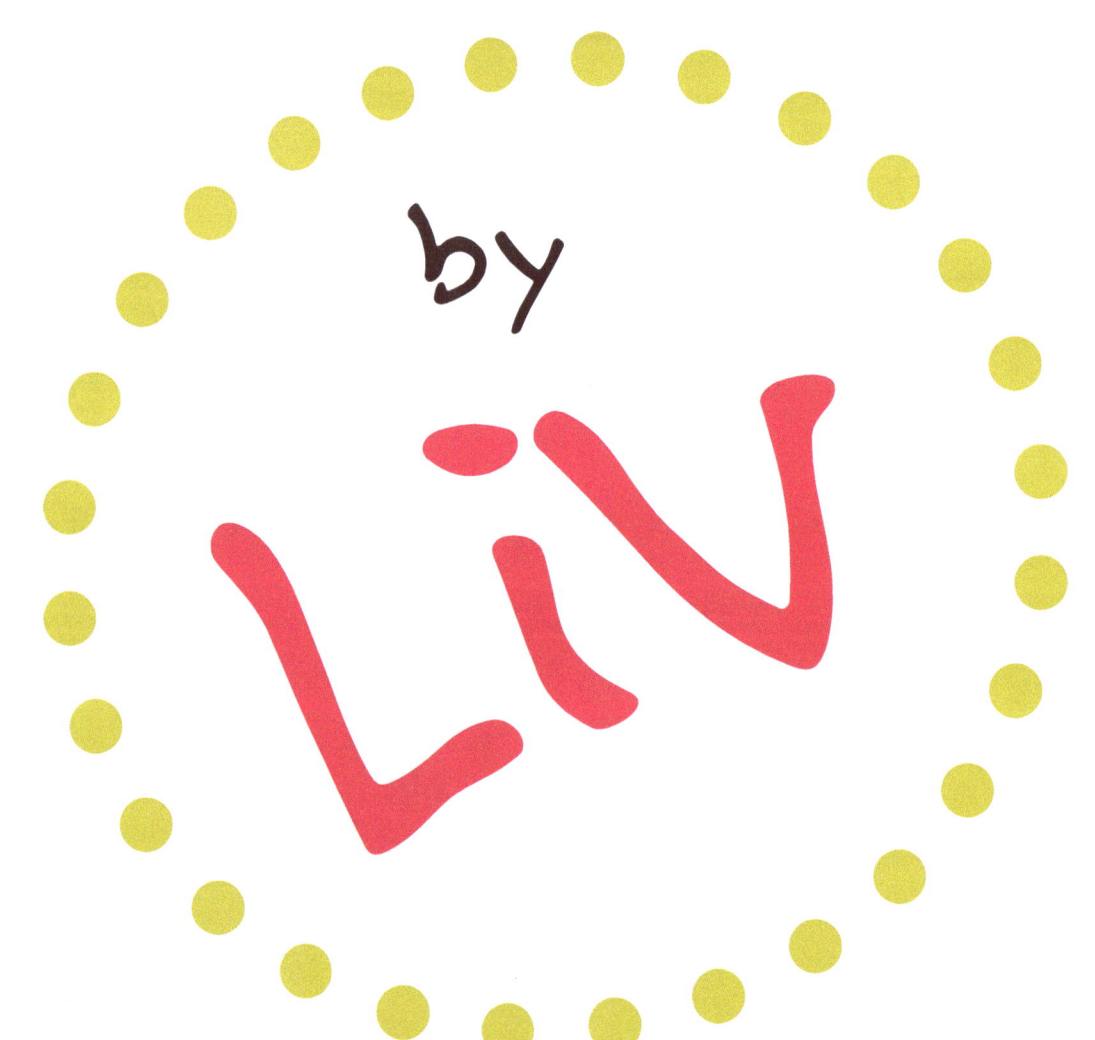

THE
CHERRY
FARM

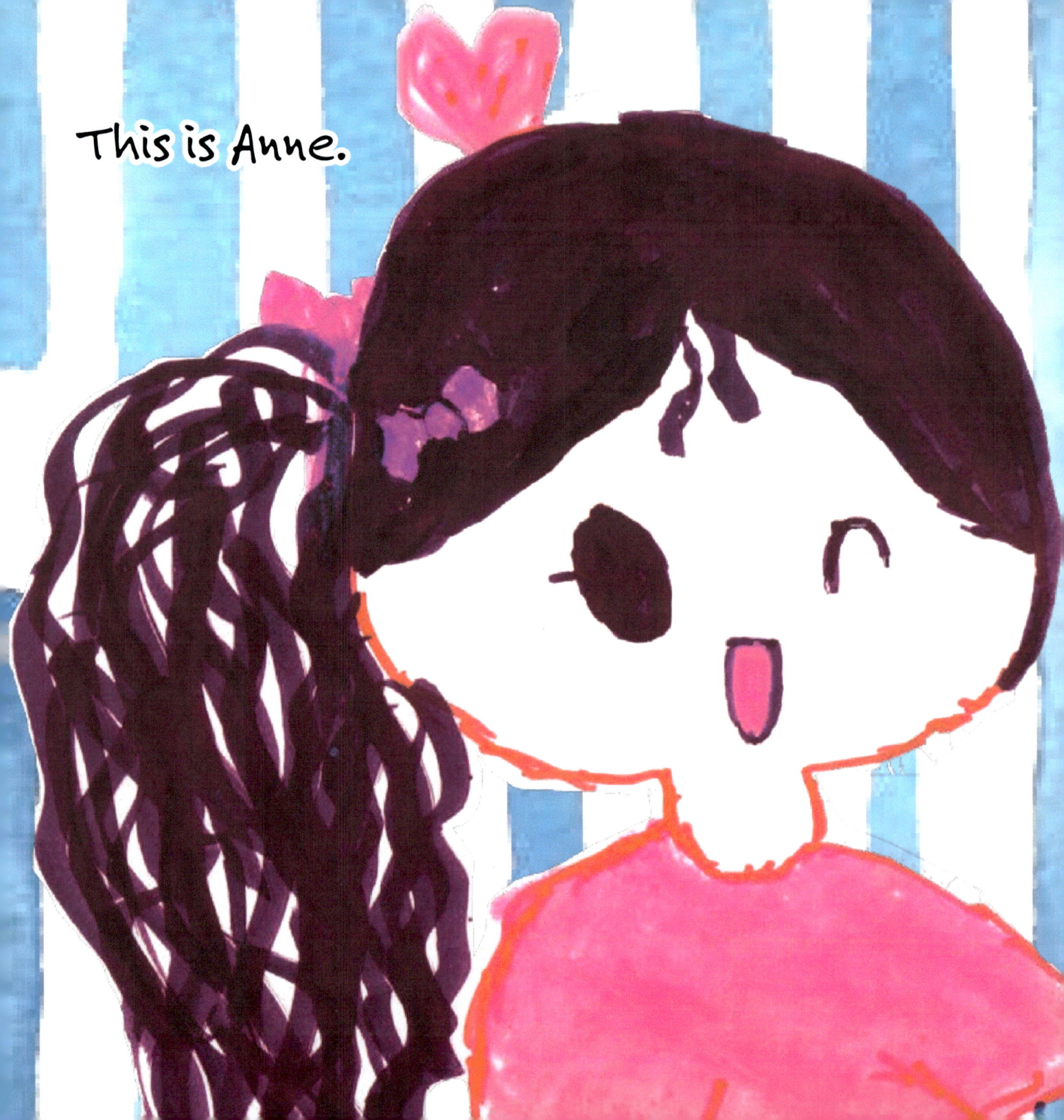

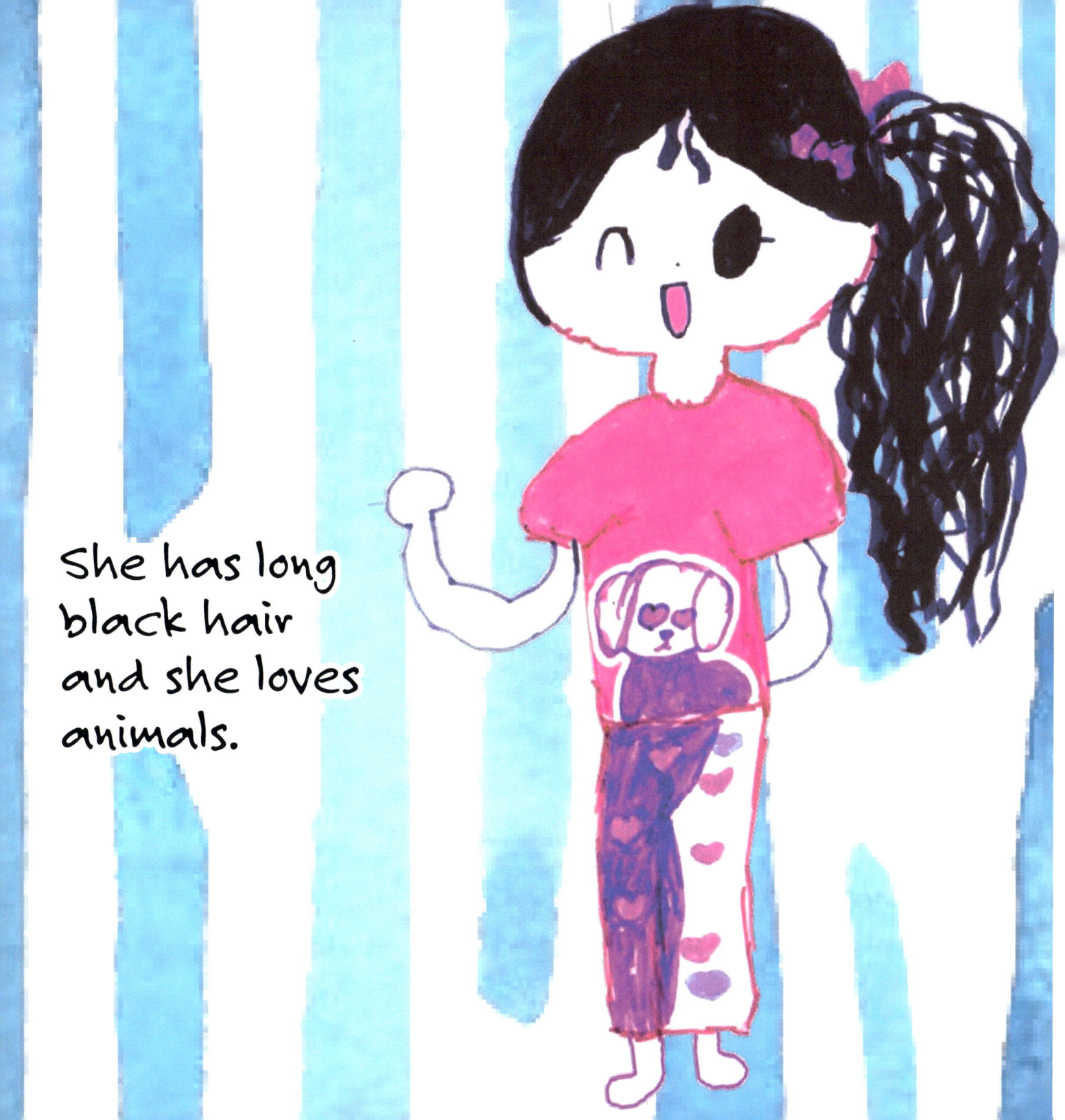

She has long black hair and she loves animals.

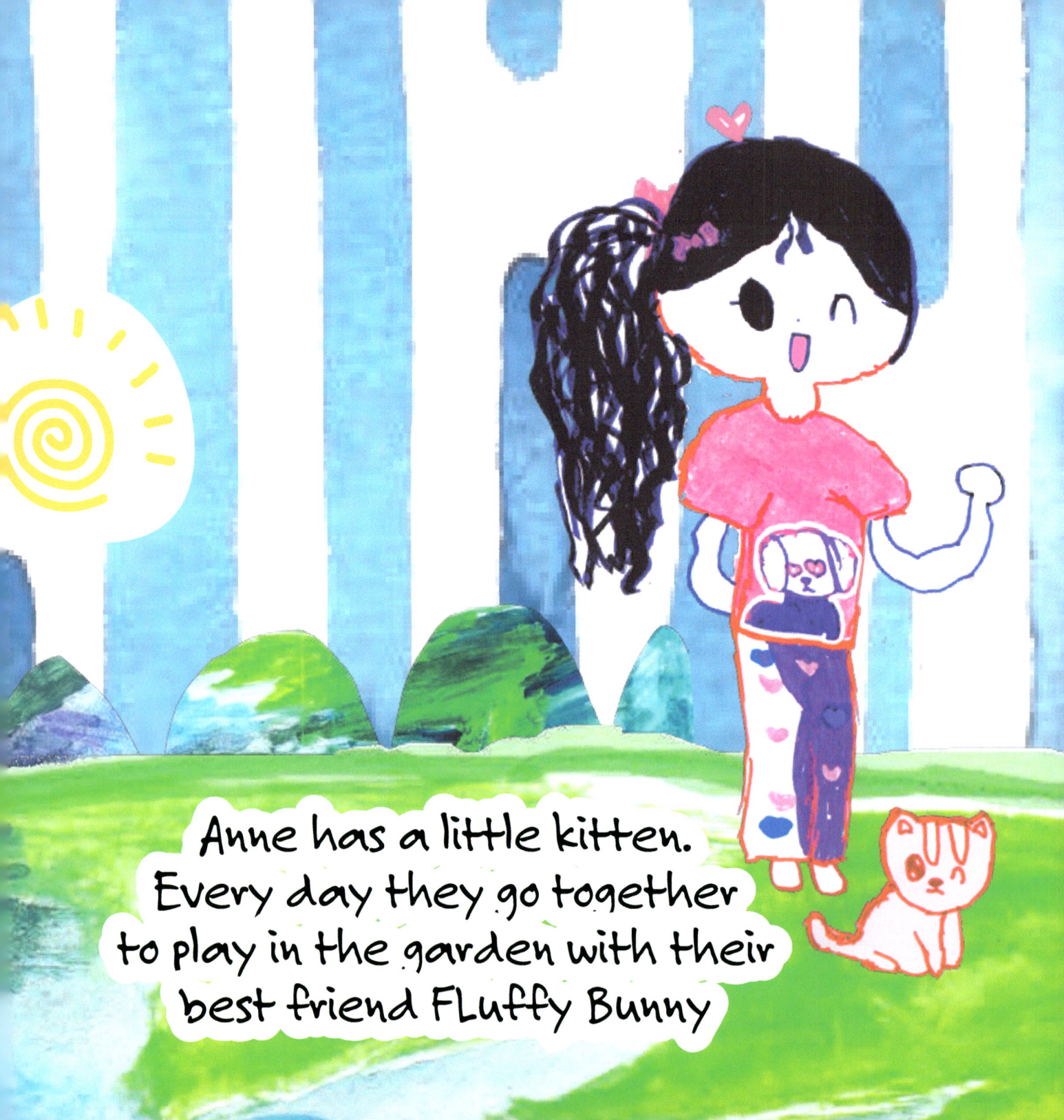

Anne has a little kitten. Every day they go together to play in the garden with their best friend Fluffy Bunny

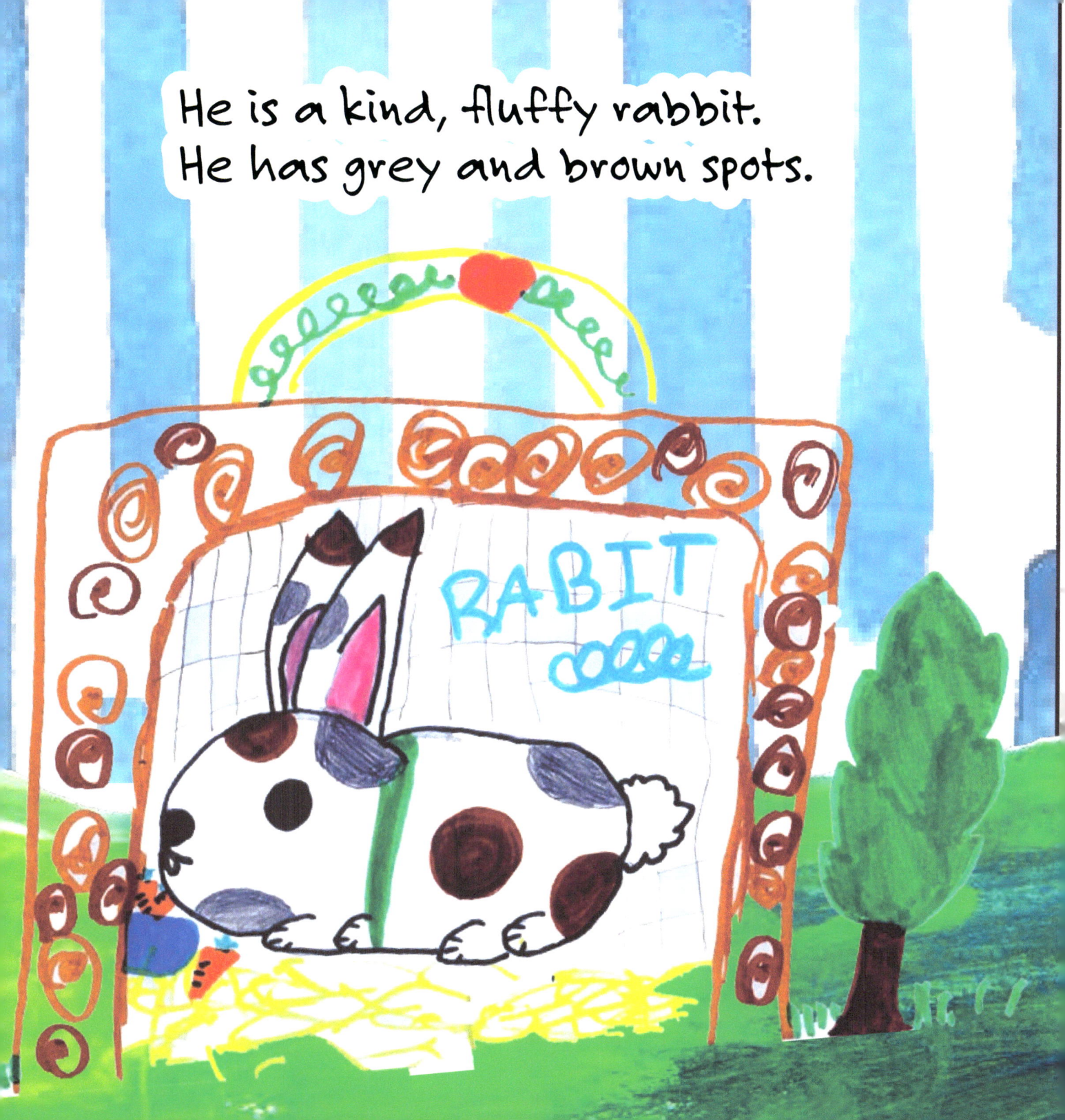

He is a kind, fluffy rabbit.
He has grey and brown spots.

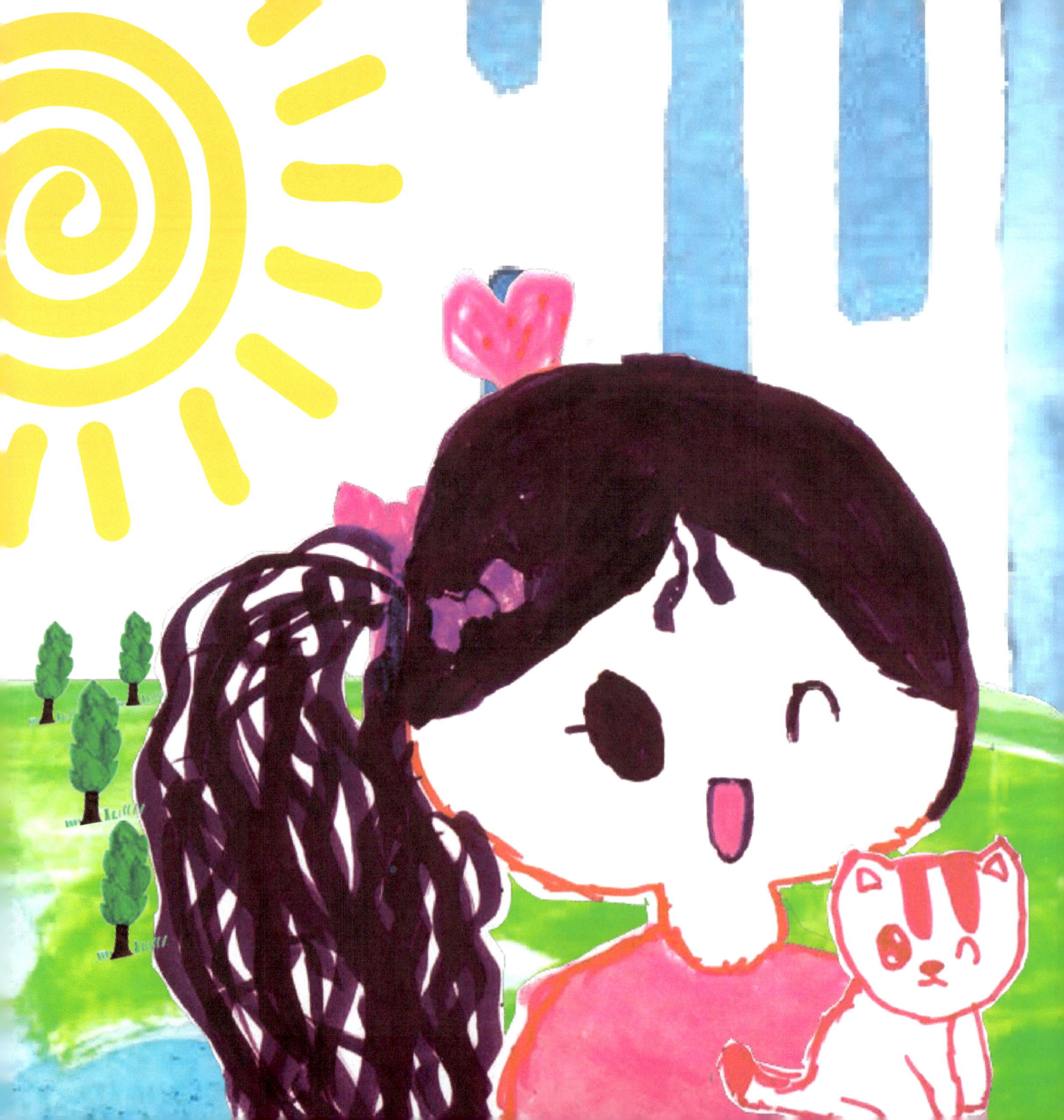

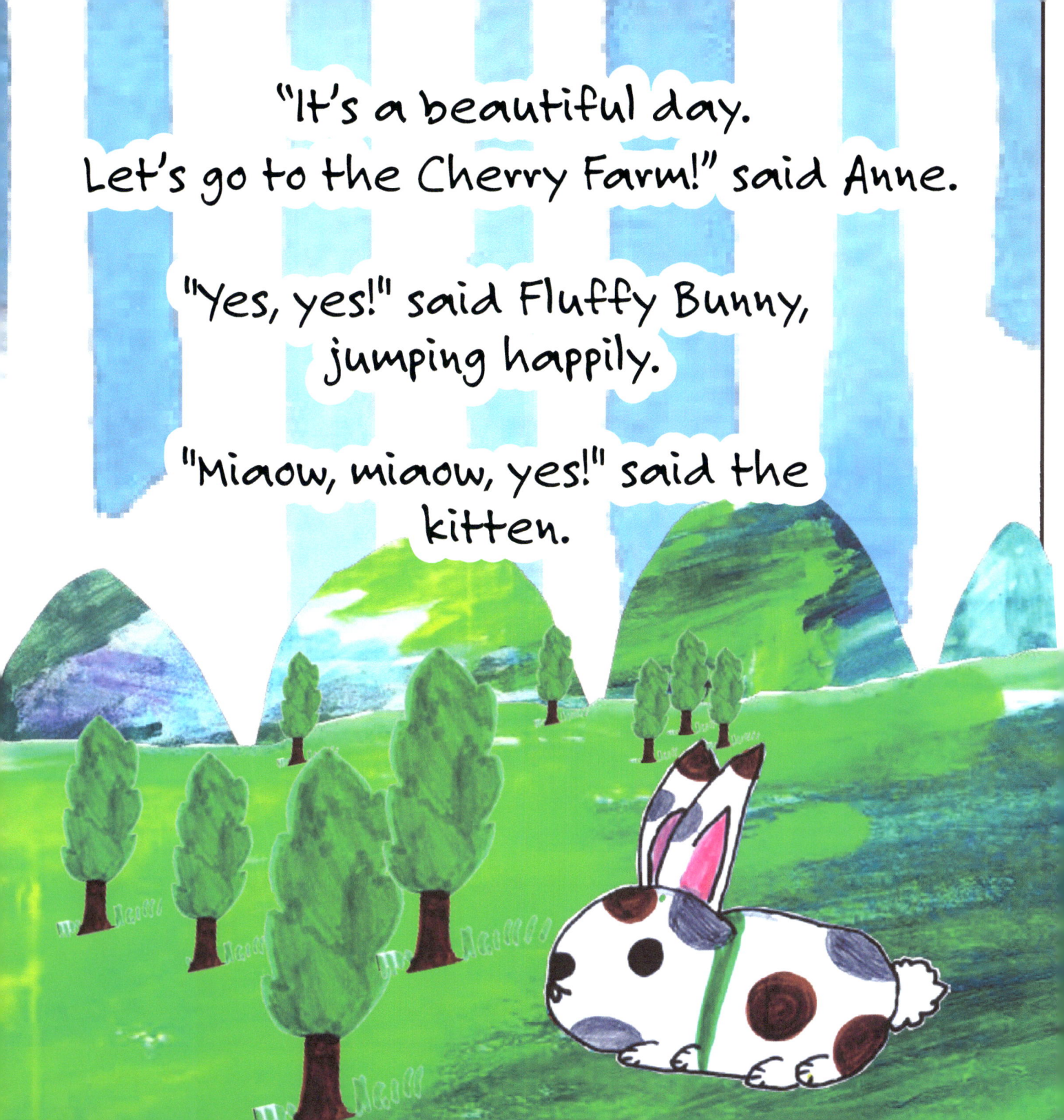

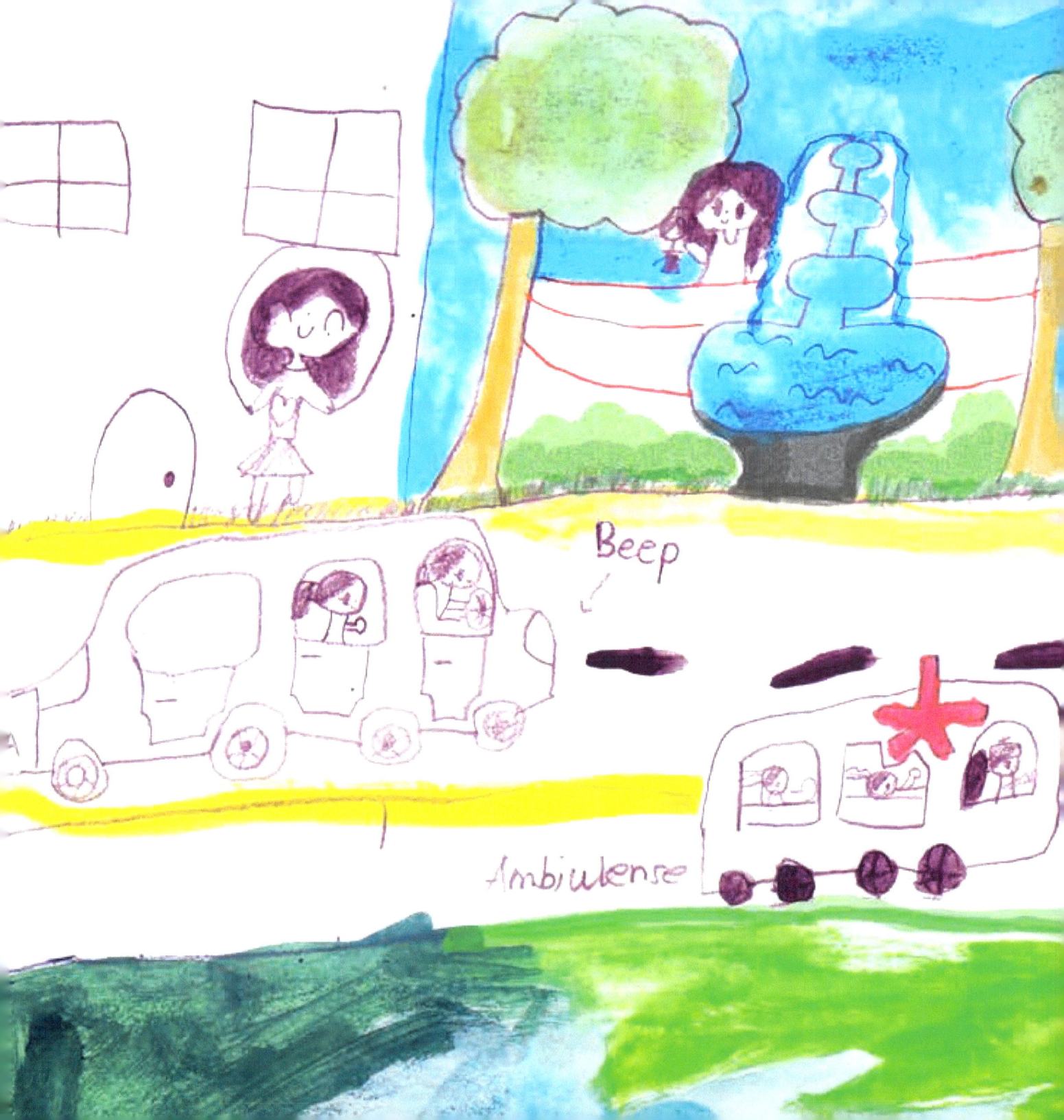

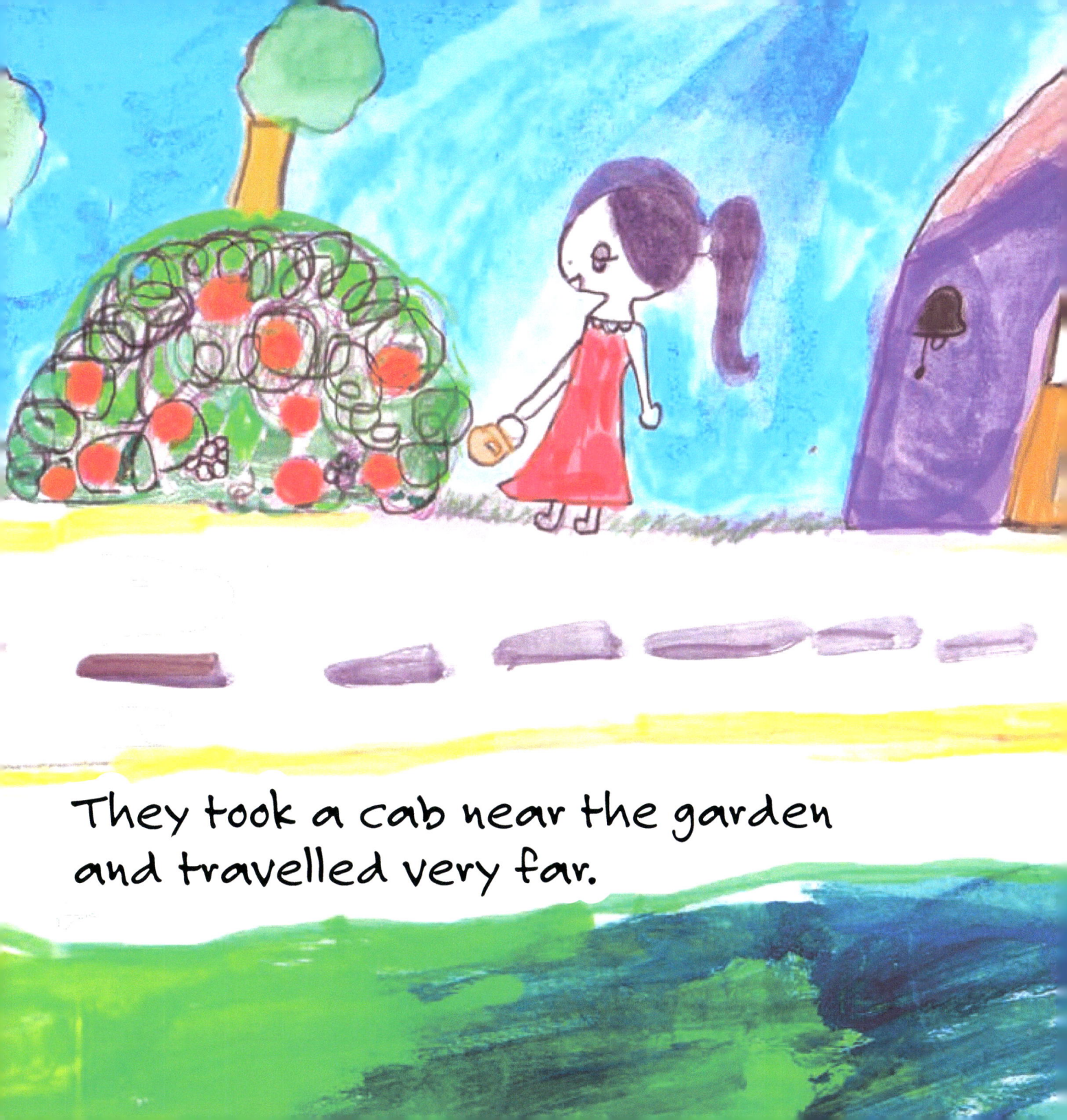

They took a cab near the garden and travelled very far.

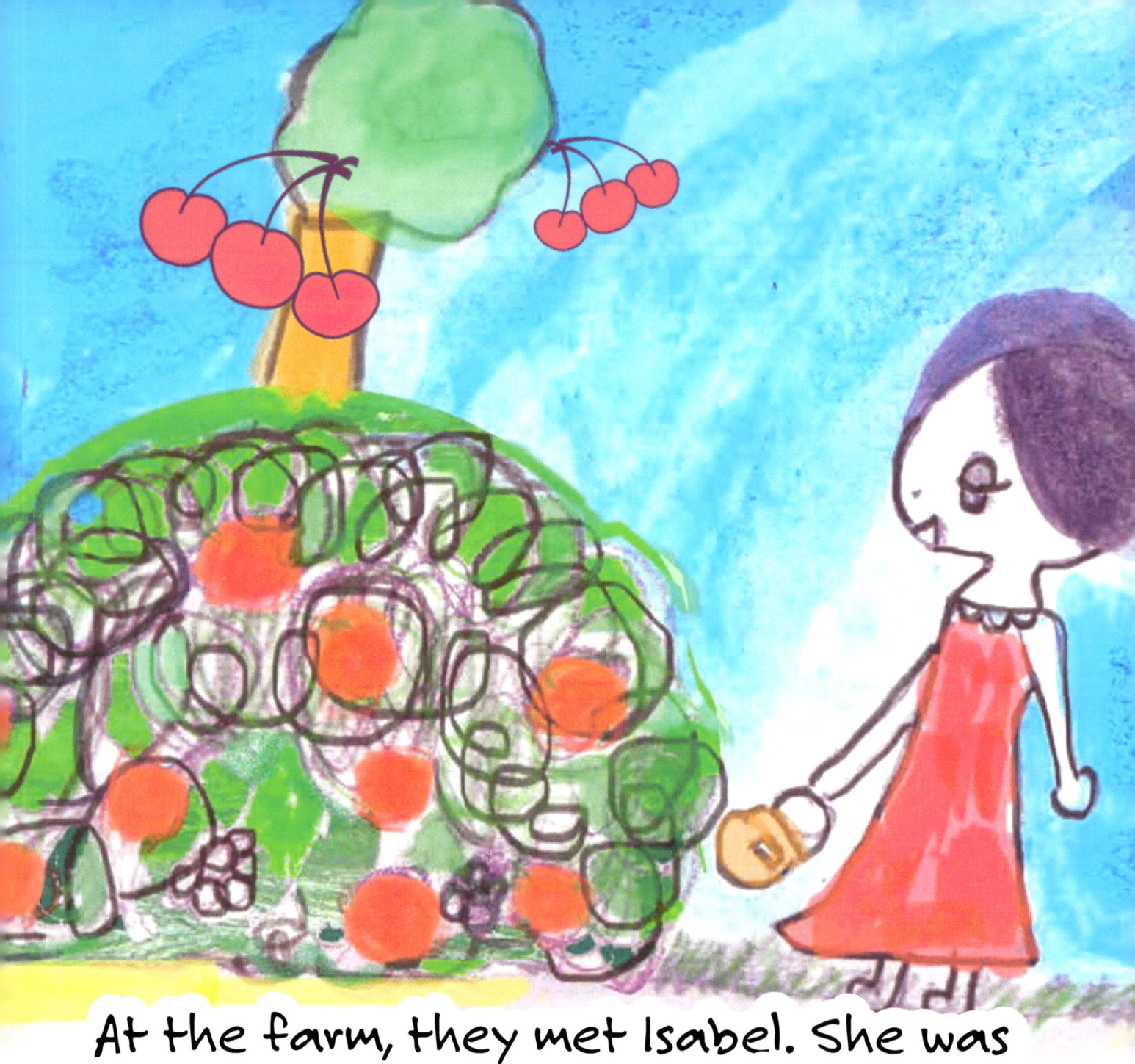

At the farm, they met Isabel. She was there picking cherries to make cupcakes.

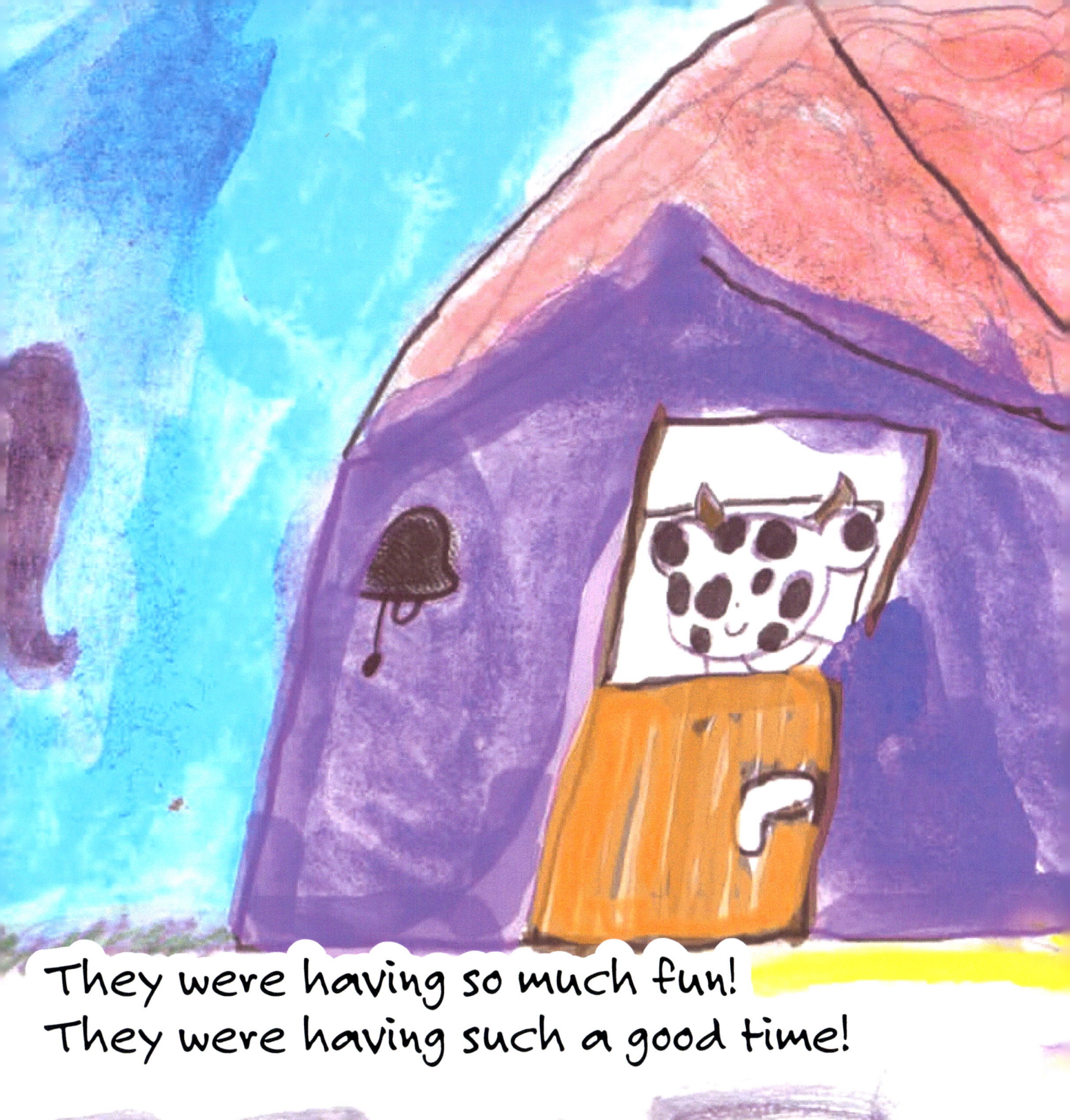

They were having so much fun!
They were having such a good time!

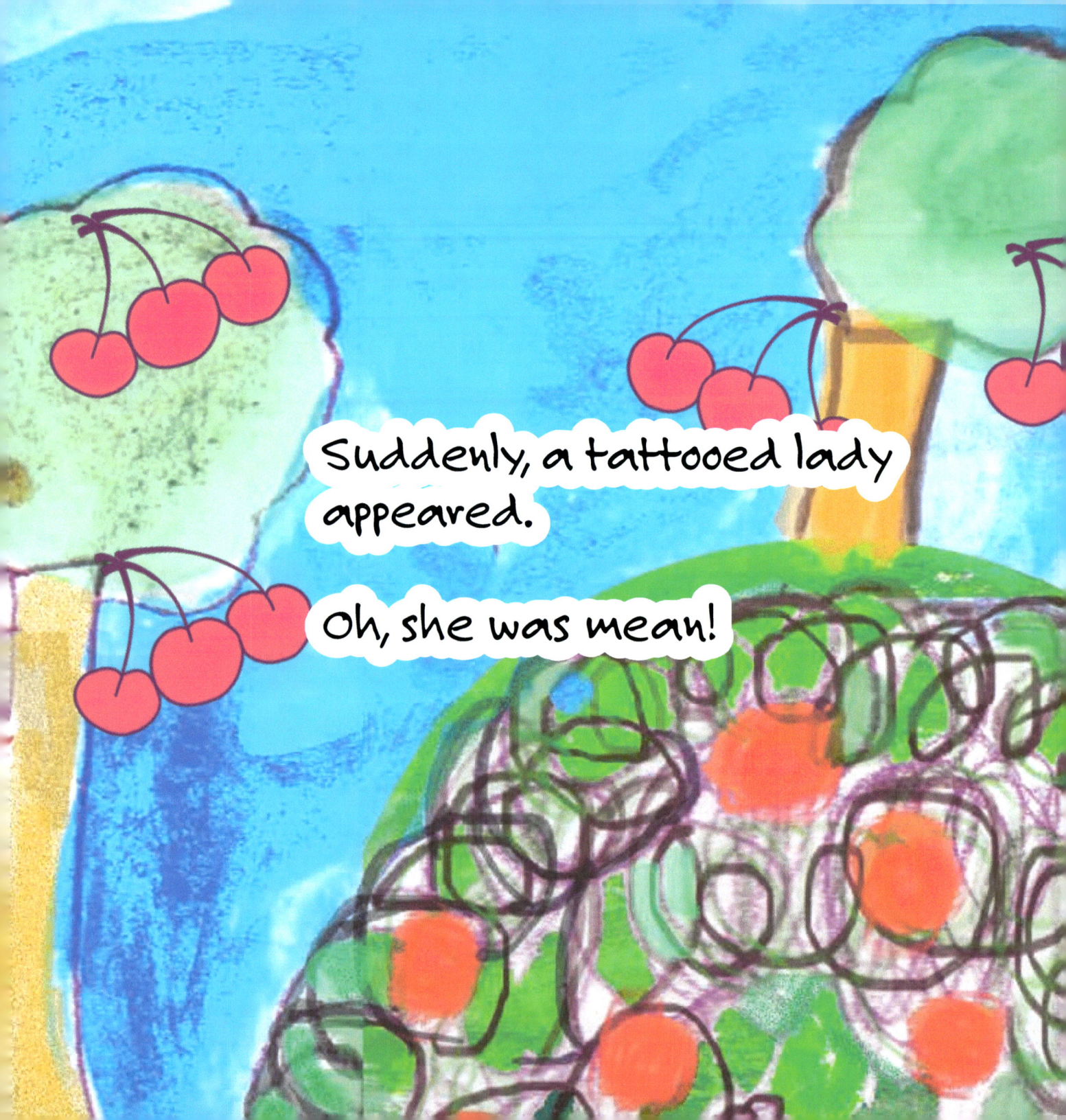

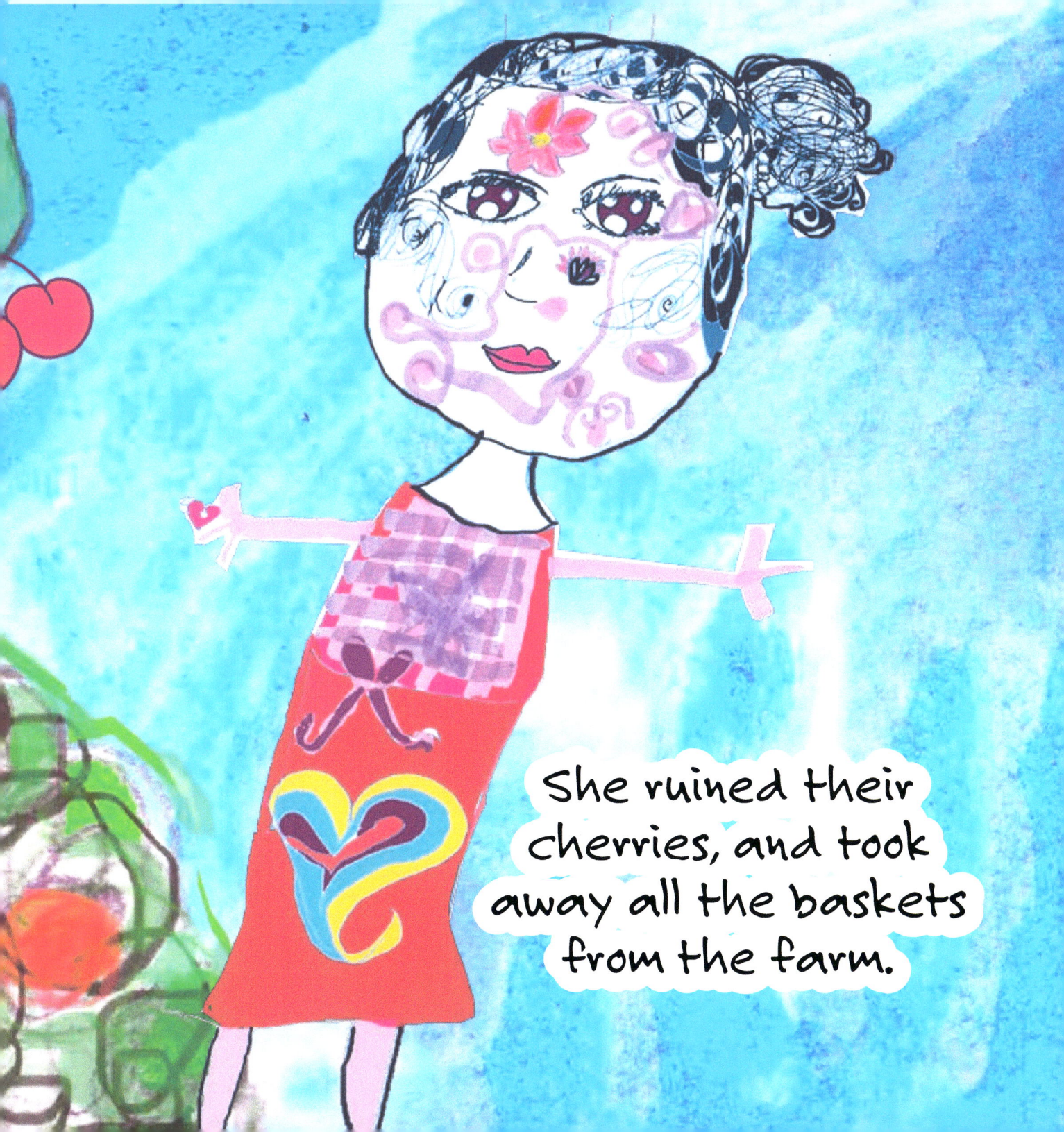

Isabel was crying!
Anne was mad!

"Let's follow her and get our cherries back", proposed the Fluffy Bunny.

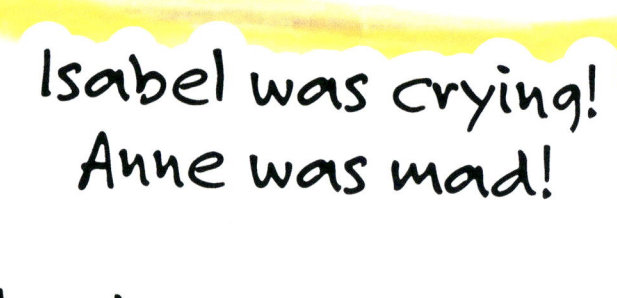

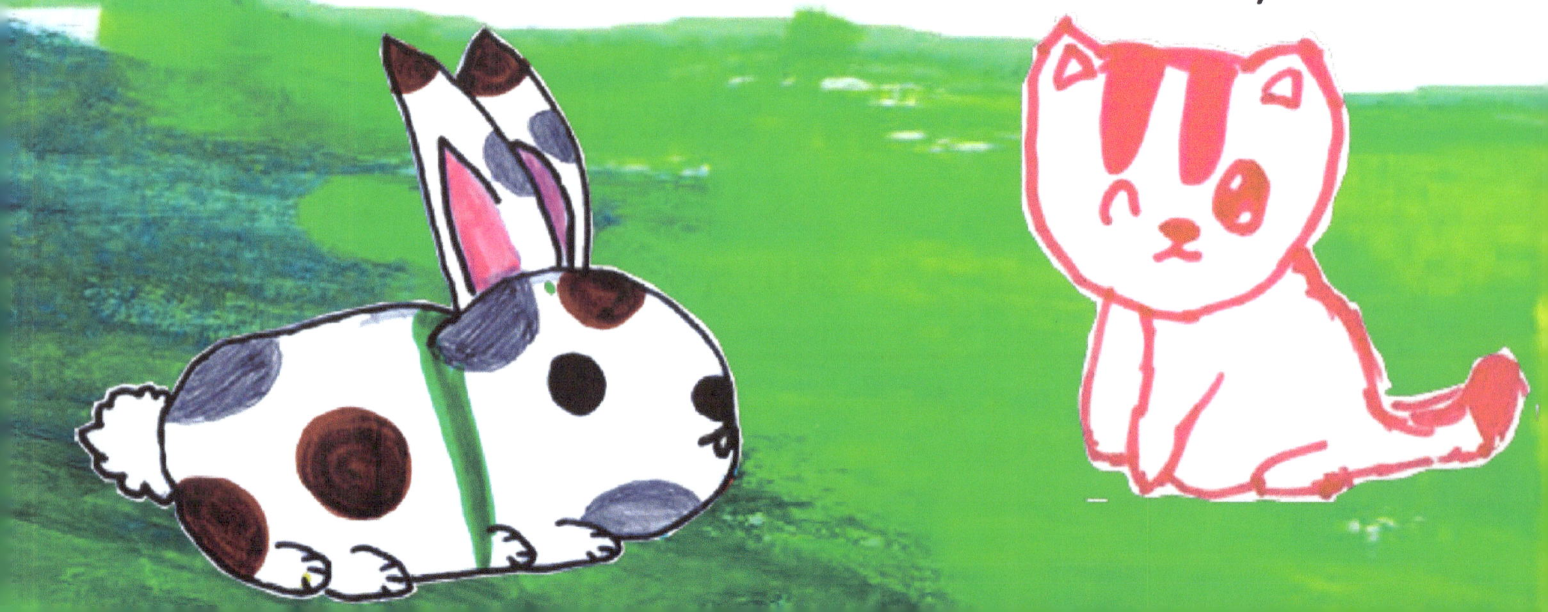

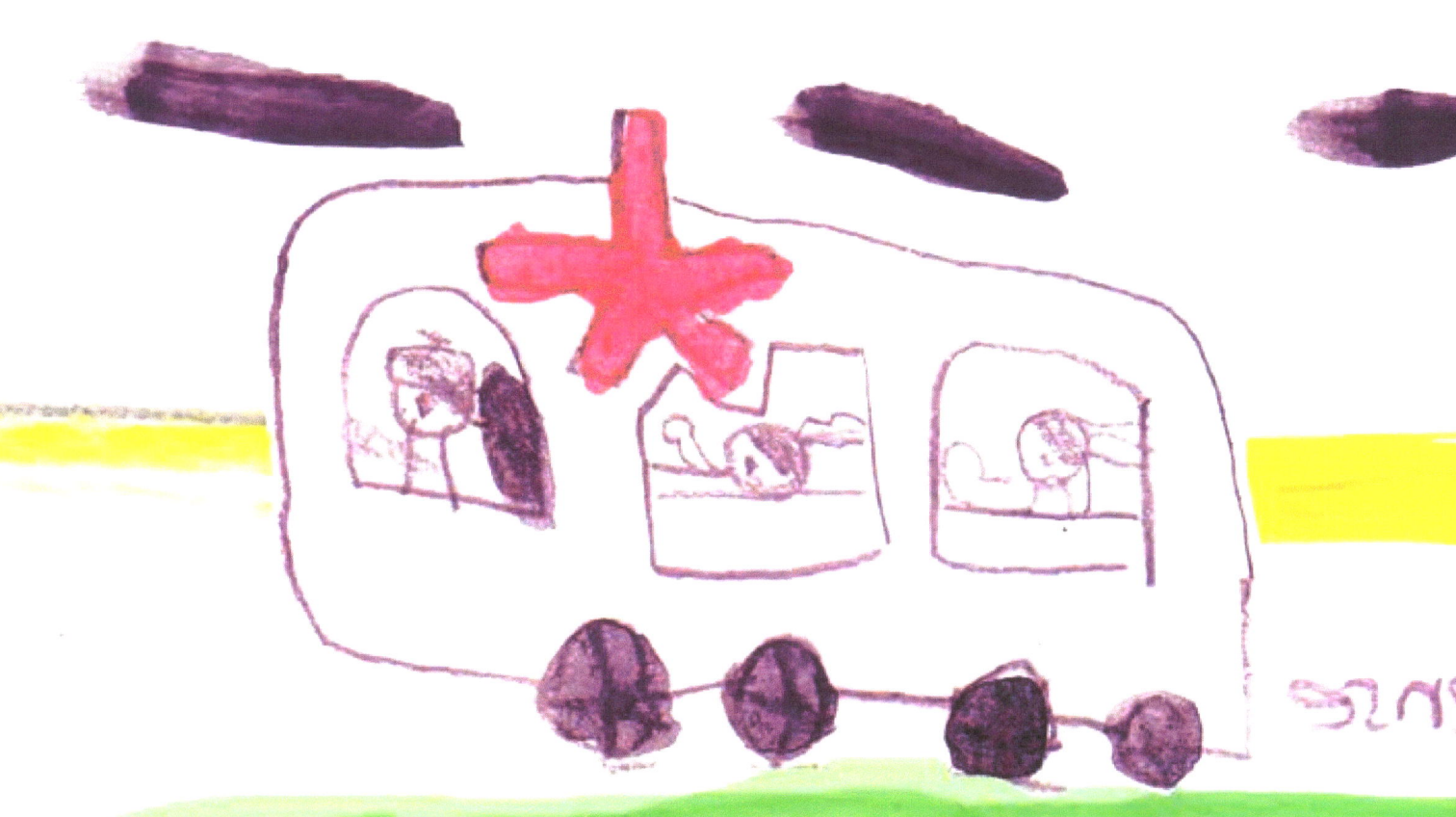

"Miaow Miaow... Yes", said the kitten.

And the ambulance driver took them to the next town.

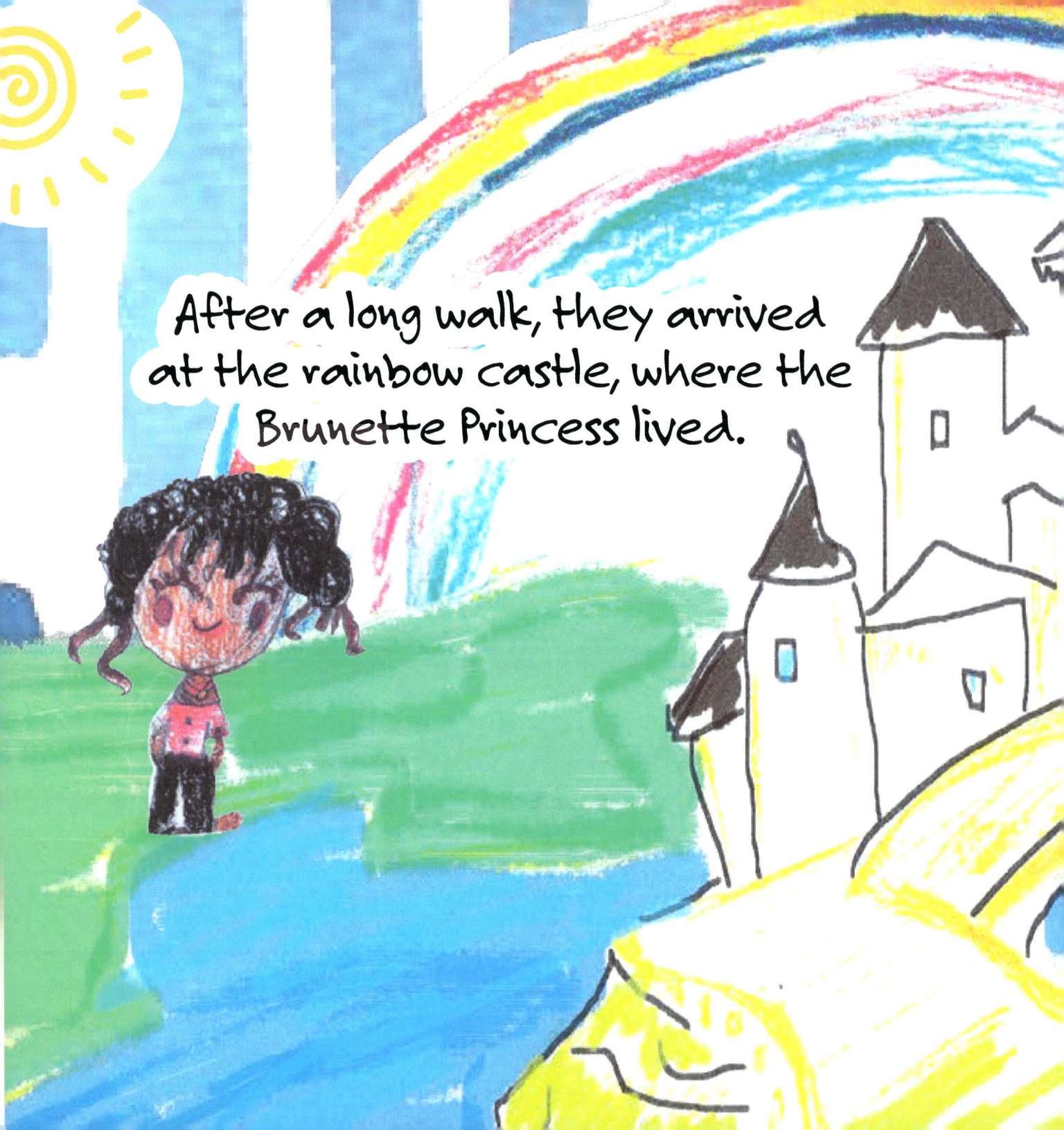
After a long walk, they arrived at the rainbow castle, where the Brunette Princess lived.

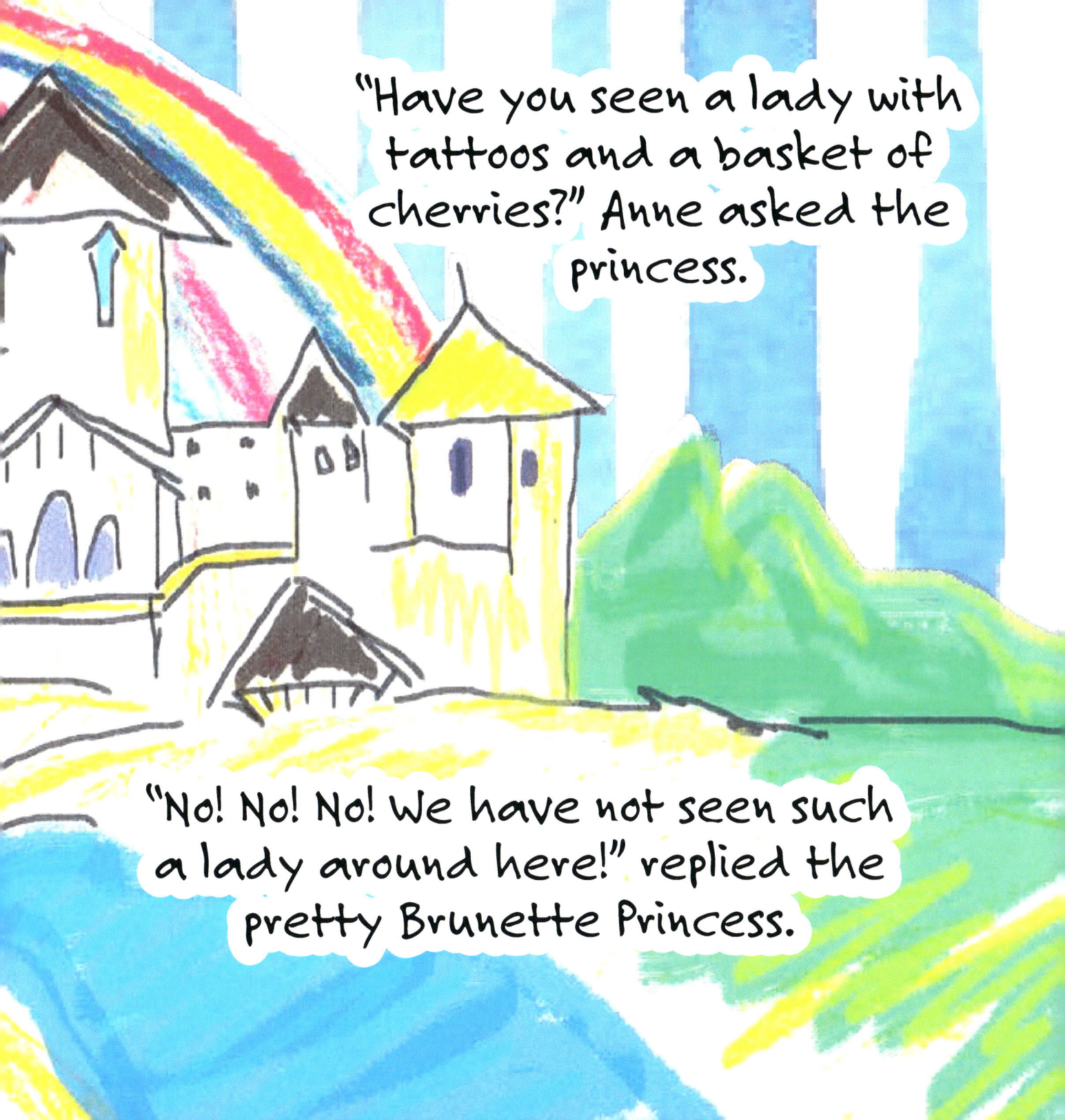

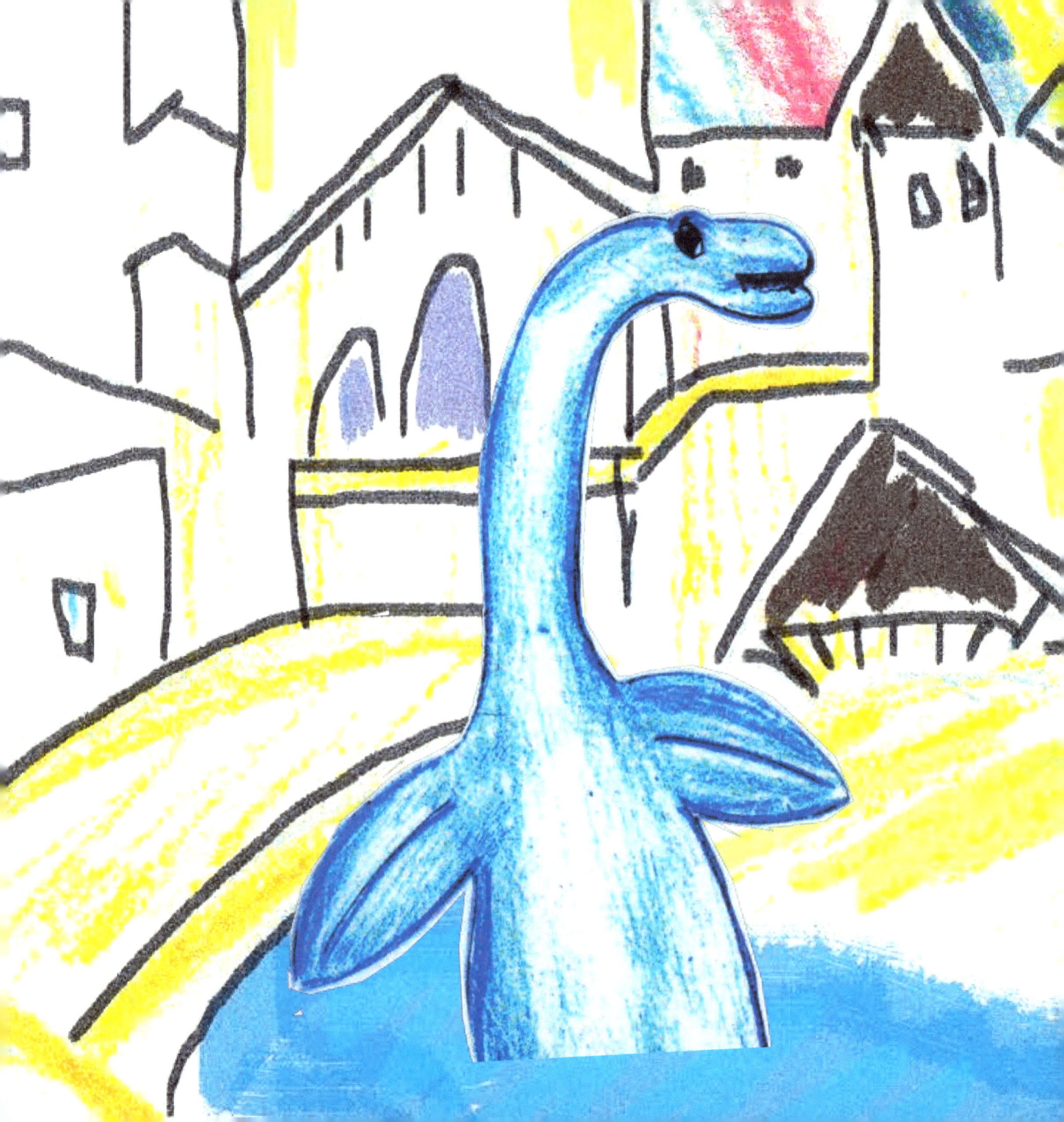

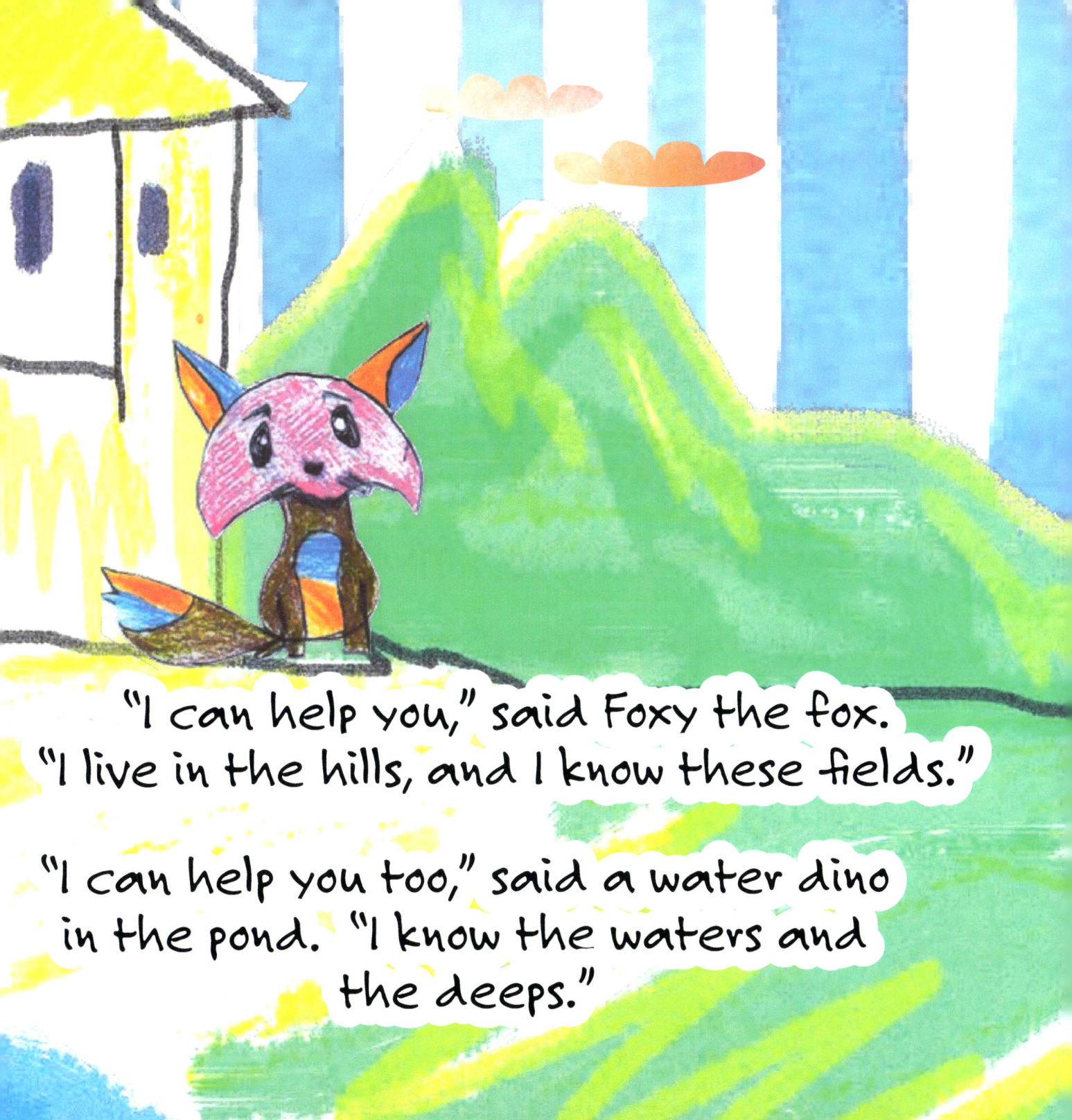

"I can help you," said Foxy the fox. "I live in the hills, and I know these fields."

"I can help you too," said a water dino in the pond. "I know the waters and the deeps."

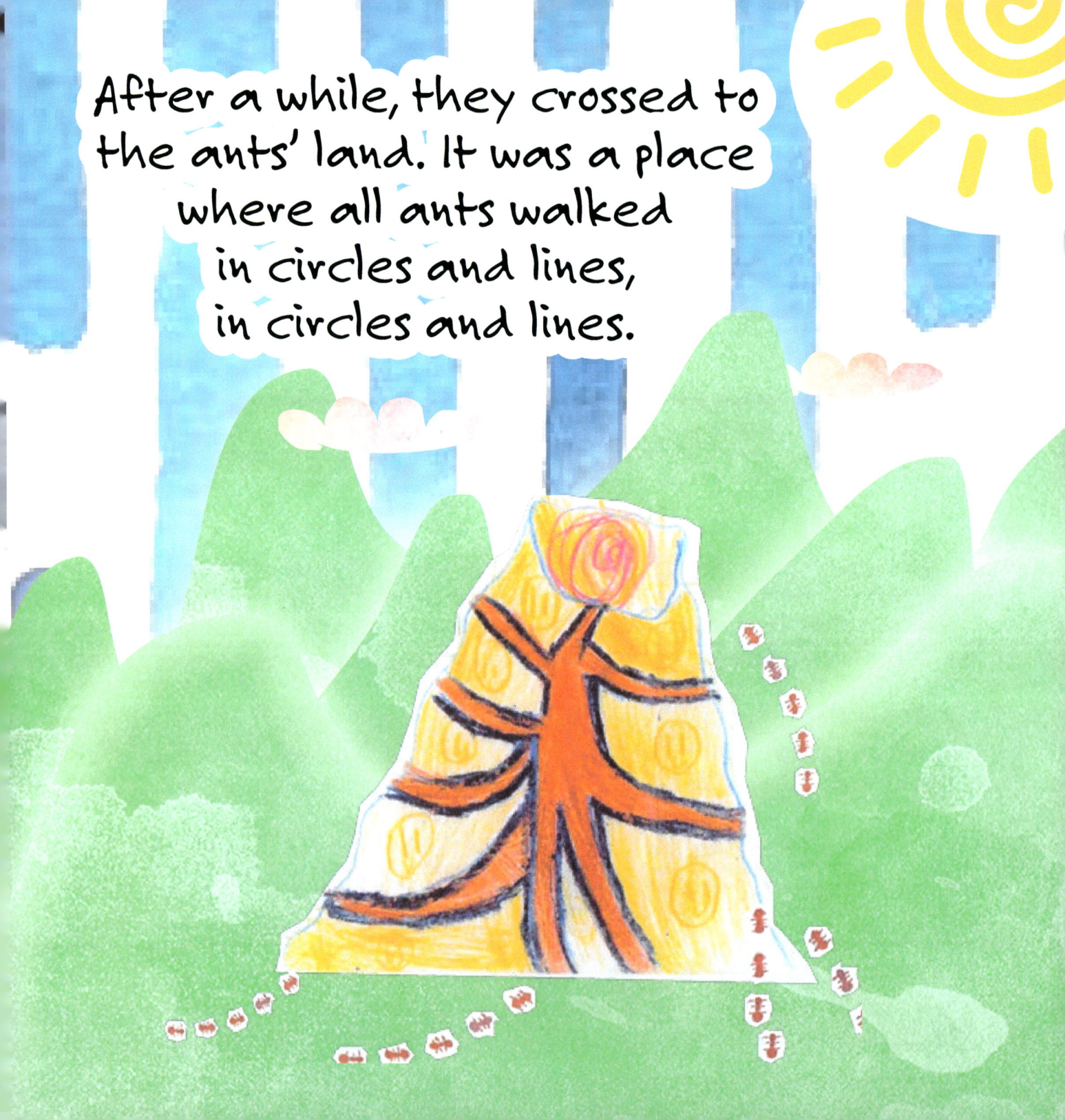

After a while, they crossed to the ants' land. It was a place where all ants walked in circles and lines, in circles and lines.

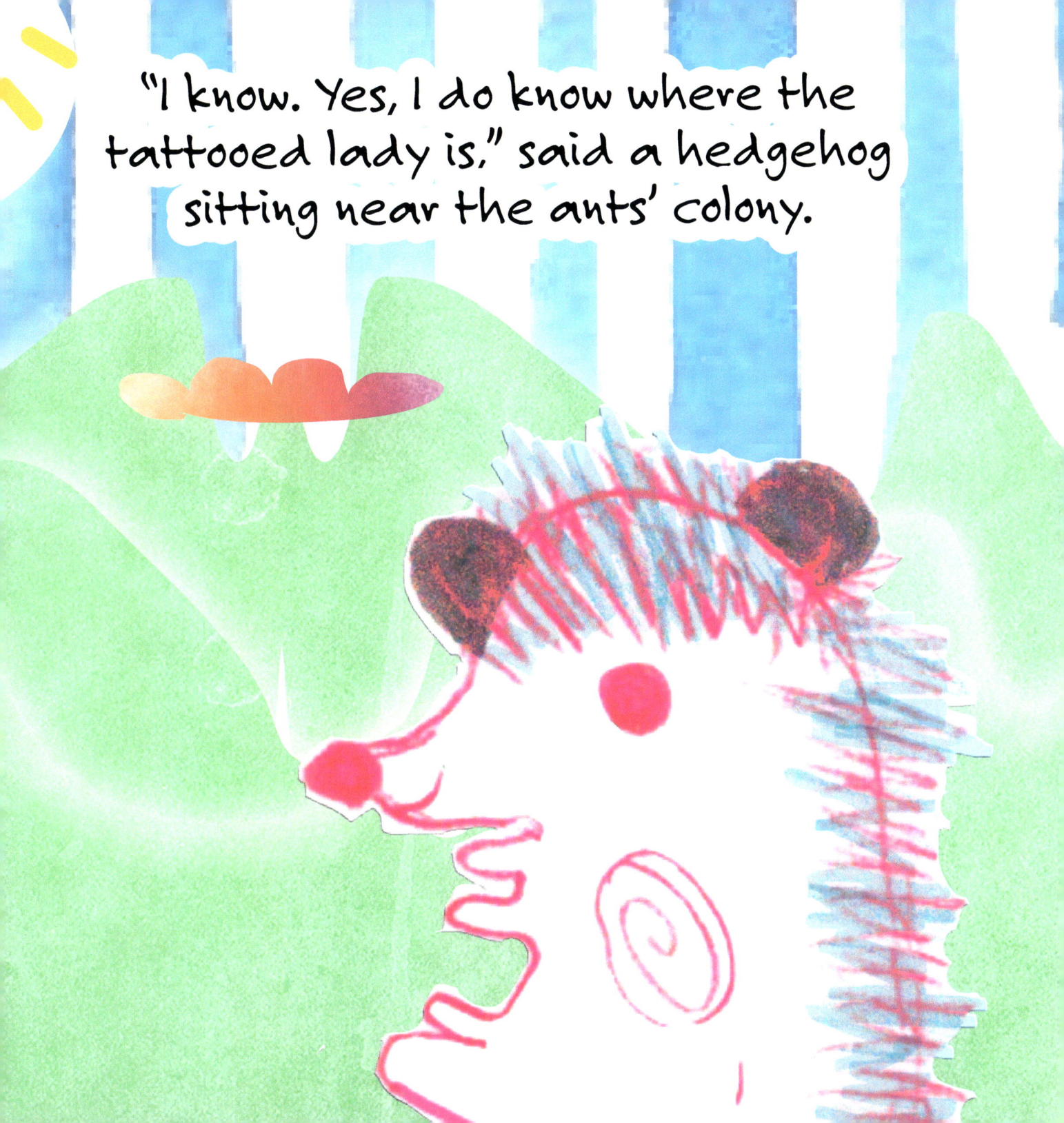
"I know. Yes, I do know where the tattooed lady is," said a hedgehog sitting near the ants' colony.

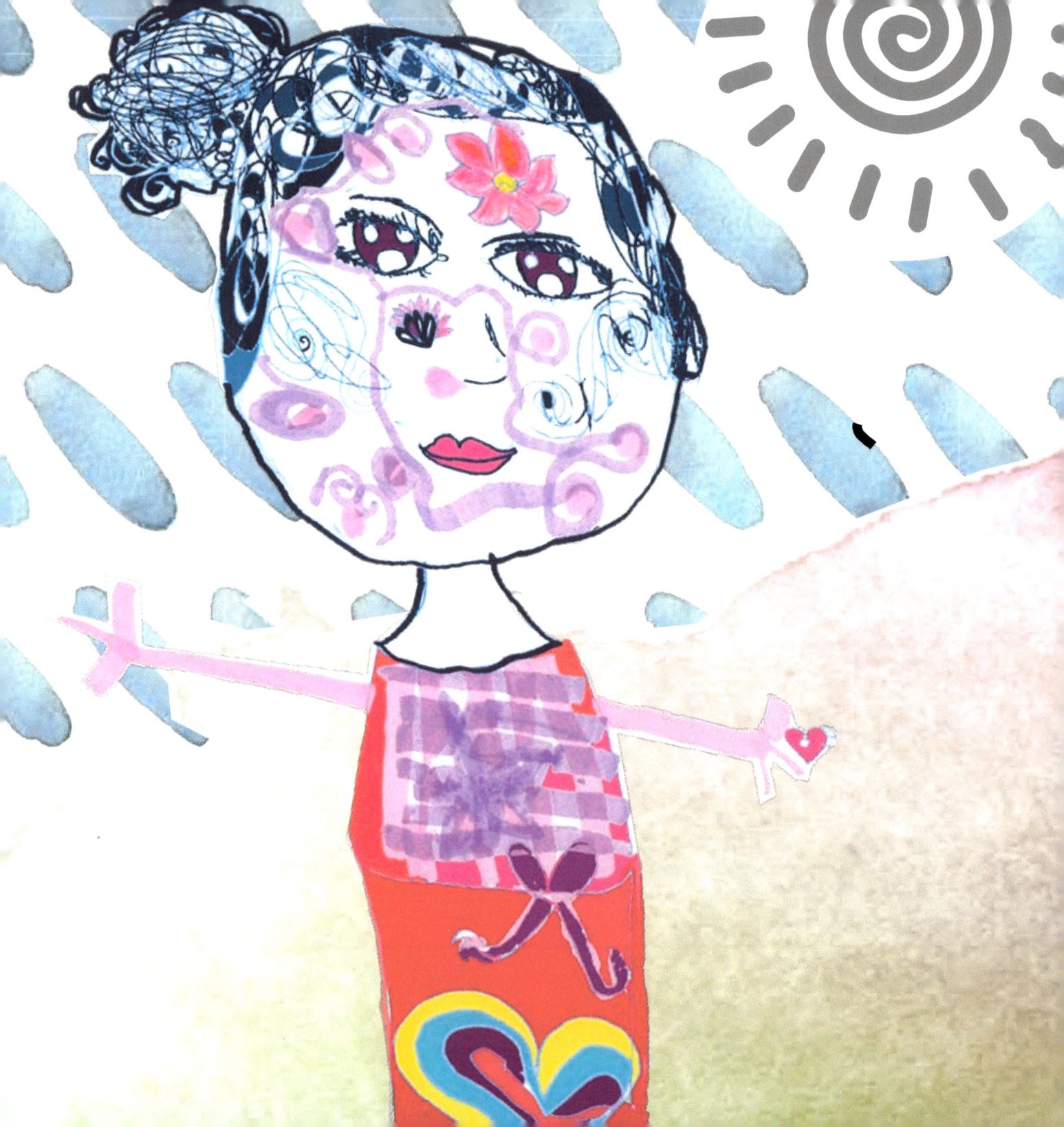

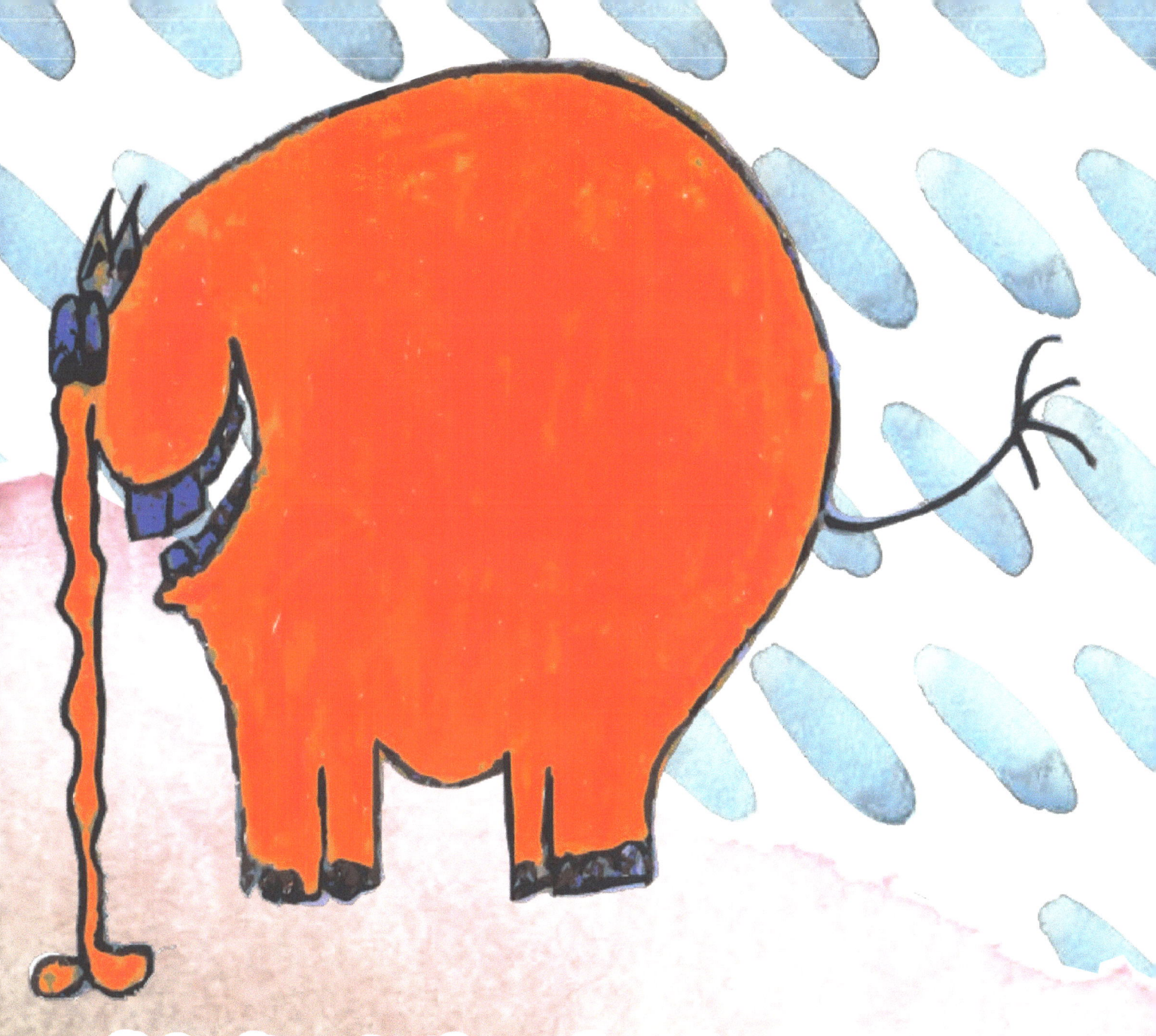

"She lives in the pale-coloured fields, with her big glutton friend, the ELEFAT."

Anne and her friends were on their way to the pale-coloured fields, when they heard a cry for help: "HELPZZZ, HELPZZZ!!!"
When Anne opened the box, she found a bee trapped inside.

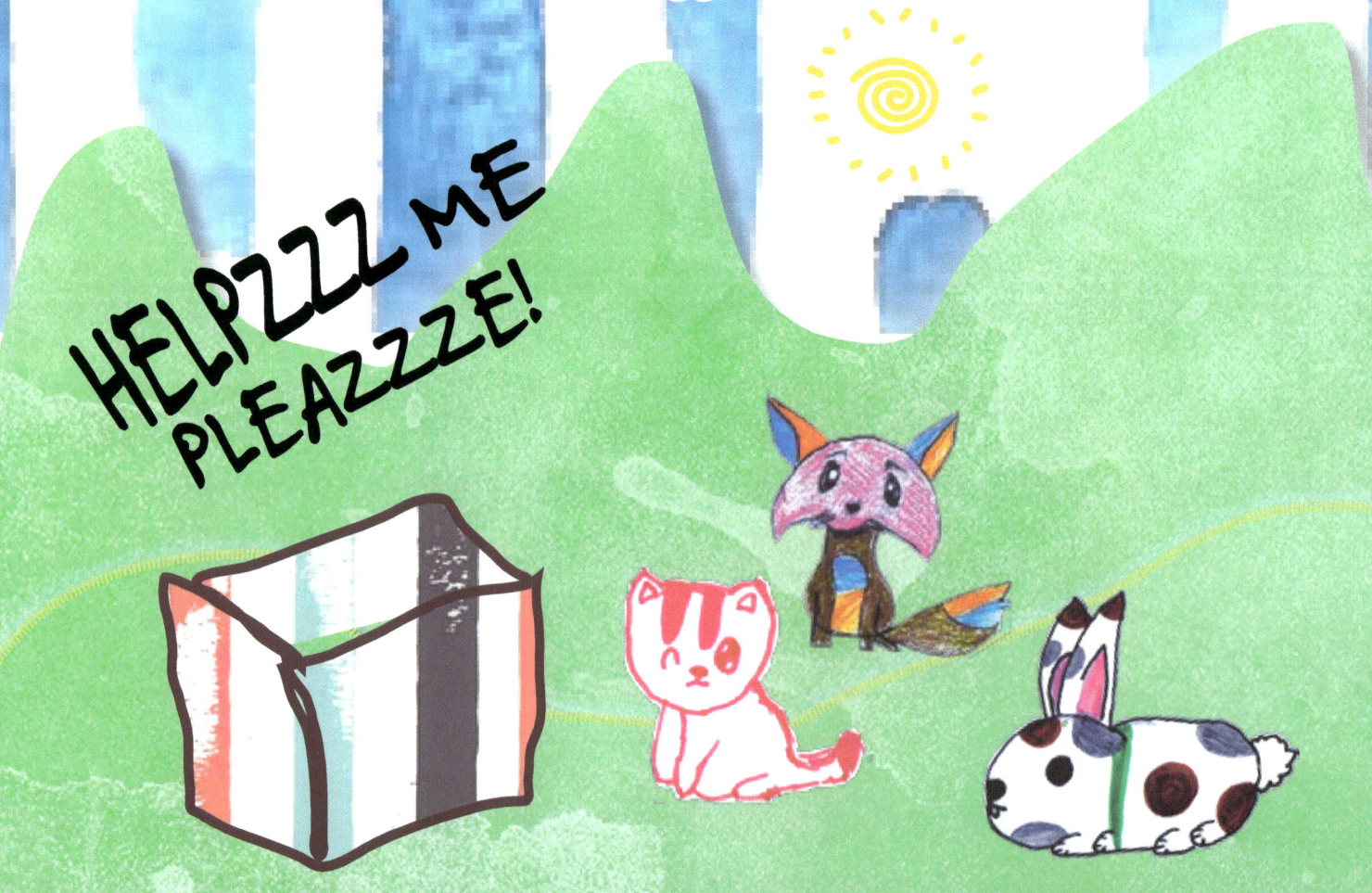

HELPZZZ ME PLEAZZZE!

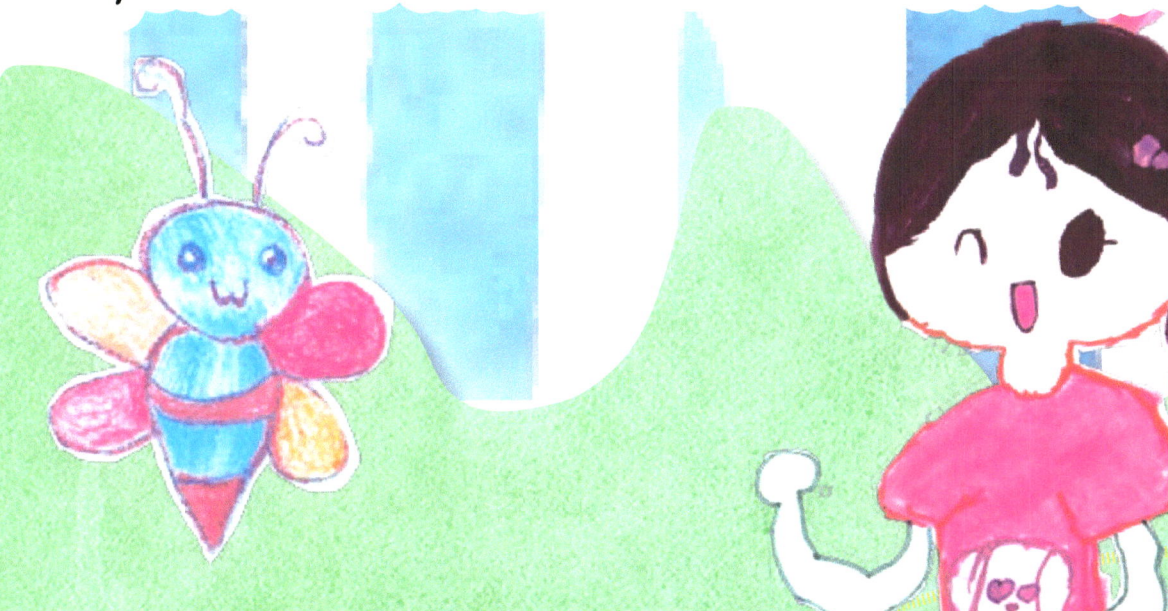

"Hi! My name is Colourful B. I was flying around when a tattooed lady locked me up."

"Oh! That lady stole our cherries too! Do you know where she is?" asked Anne.

"No, I do not know. But I saw a basket of cherries inside the fallen tree," said B.

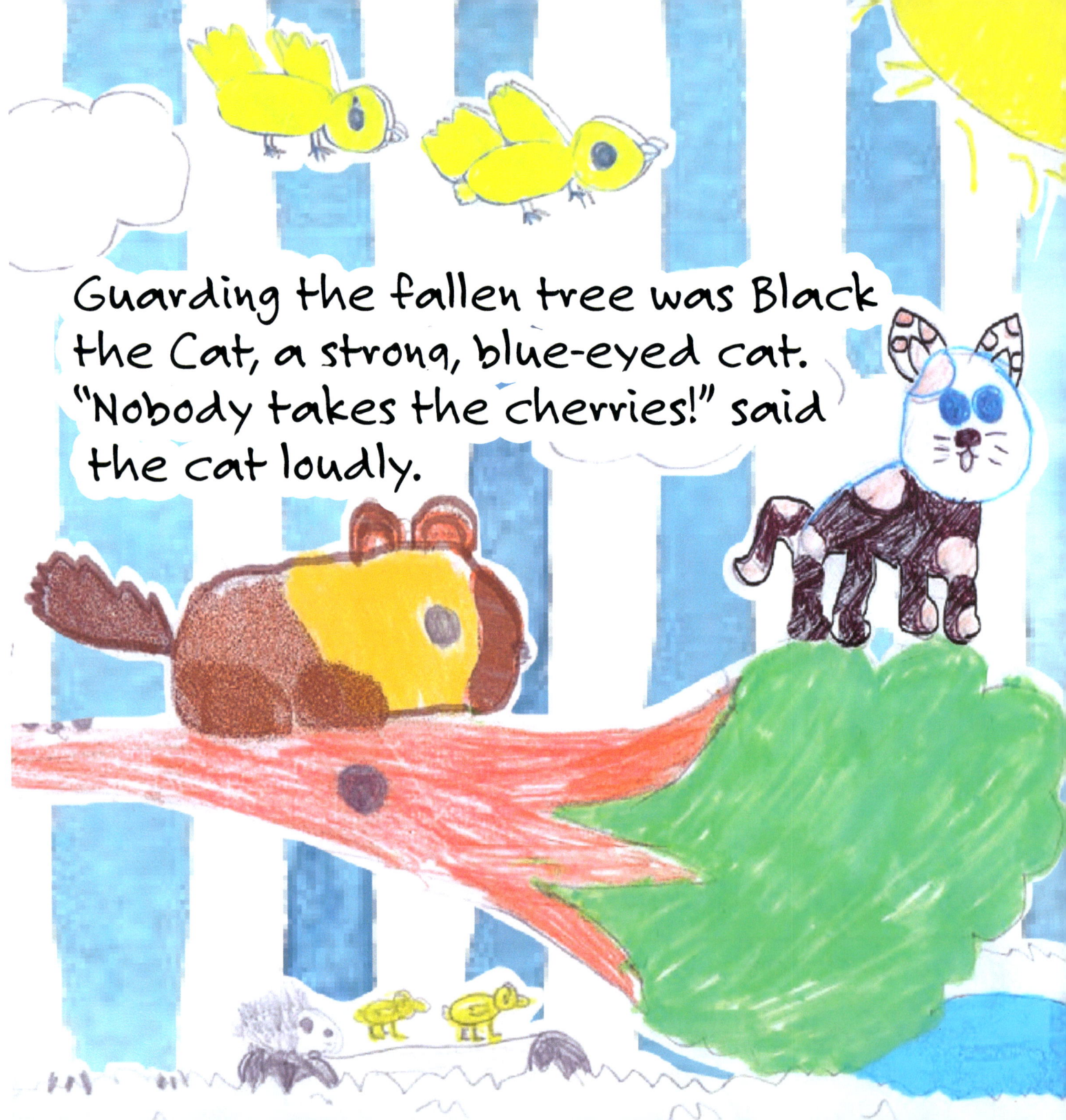

Anne was afraid, and cried for help. All the animals heard her and came to help. Scared of the fox and the giant water dino, Black the Cat ran away.

"Quickly, quickly! Take the basket of cherries now, before the tattooed lady comes back," said a blue hummingbird.

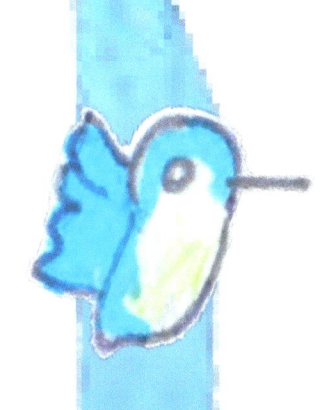
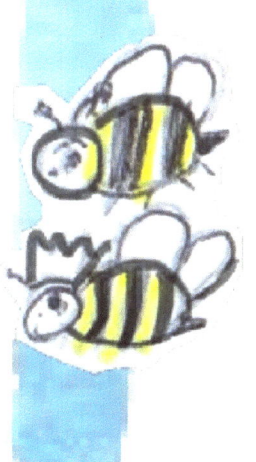
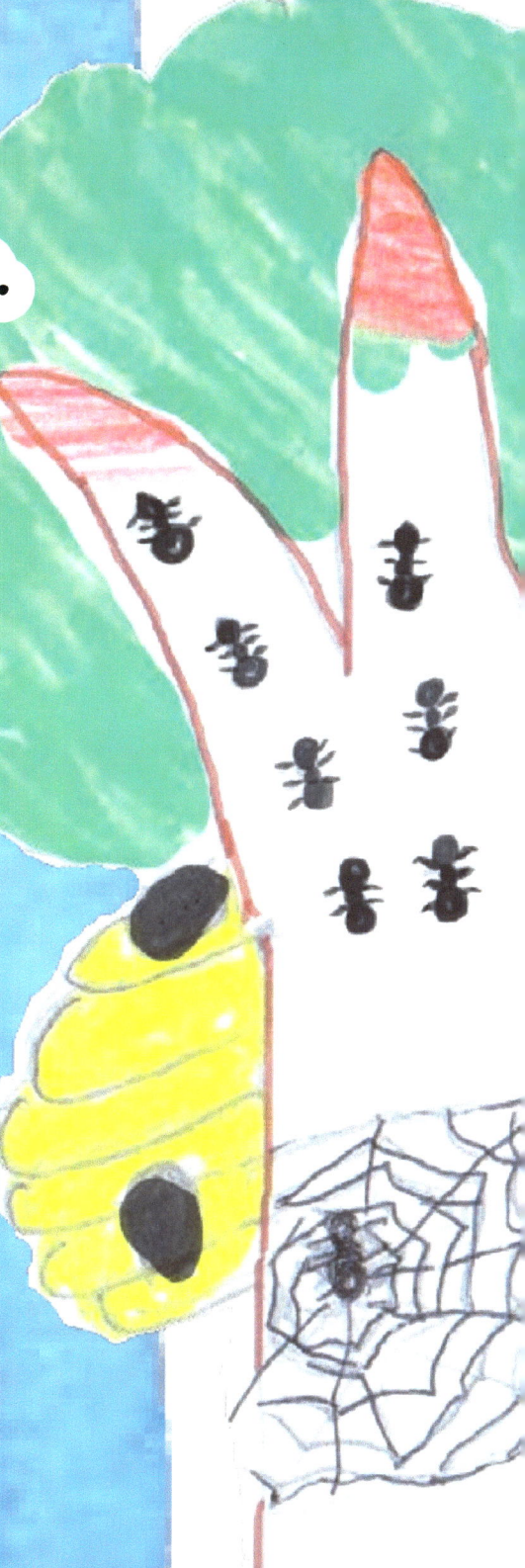

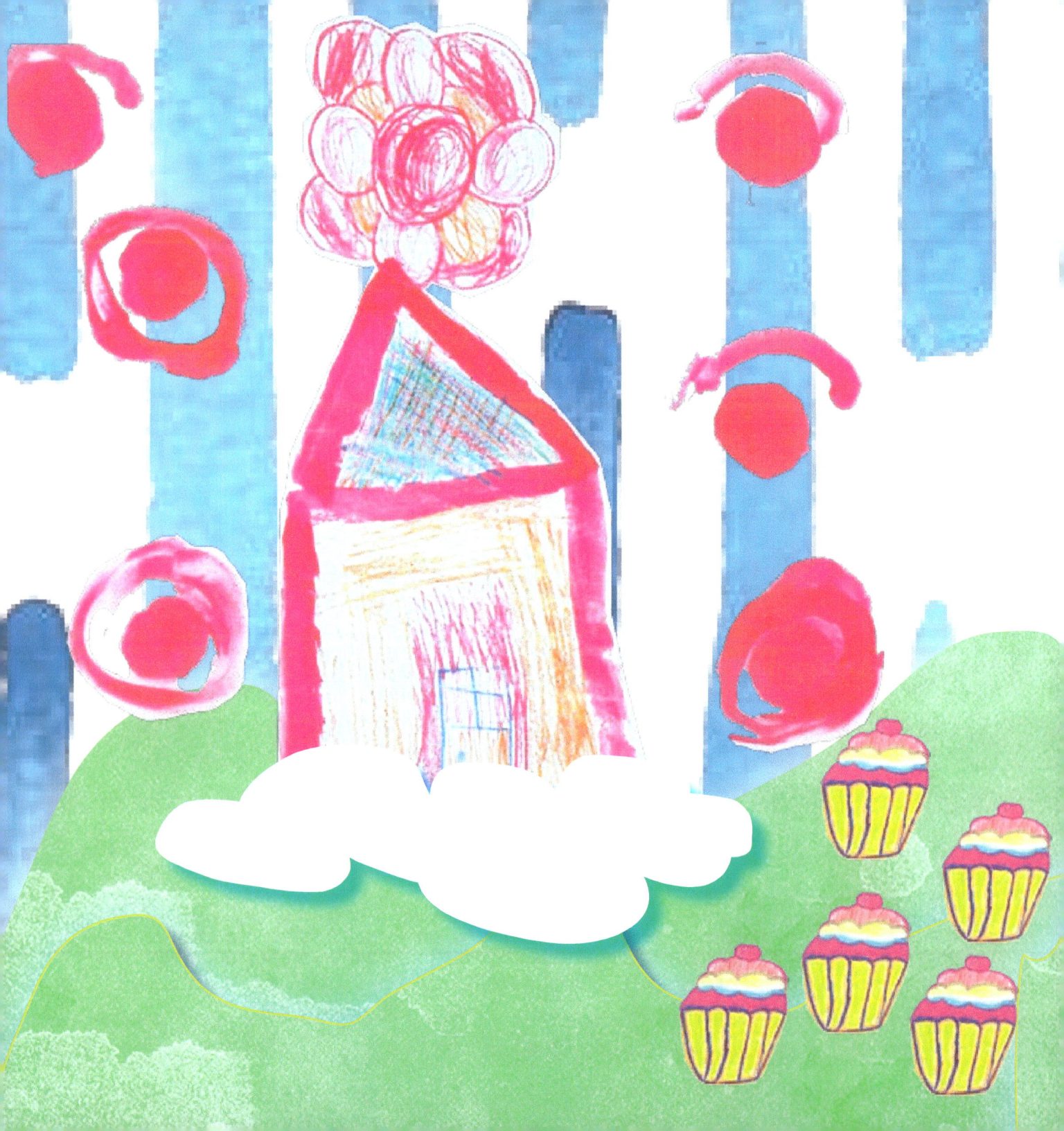

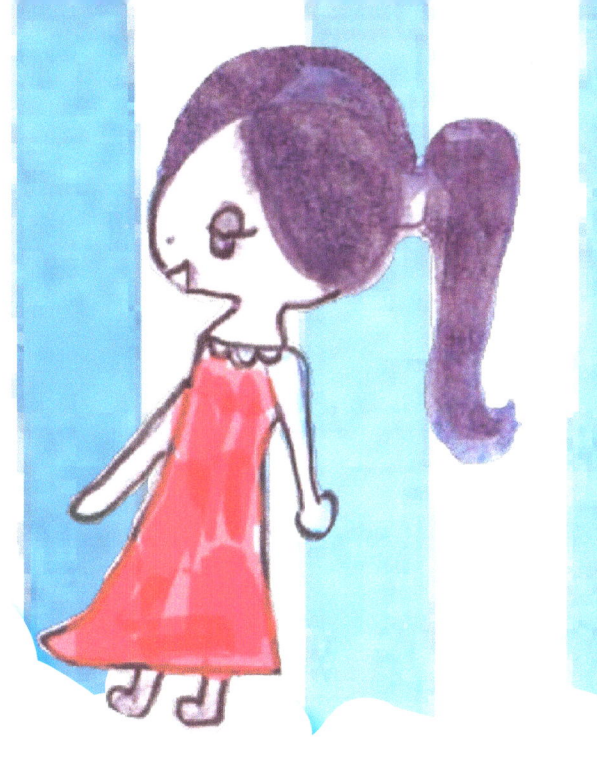

They got the basket of cherries back!

Isabel was very, very happy.
She went to her balloon house, on the green mountain clouds, and she cooked cherry cupcakes for everyone.

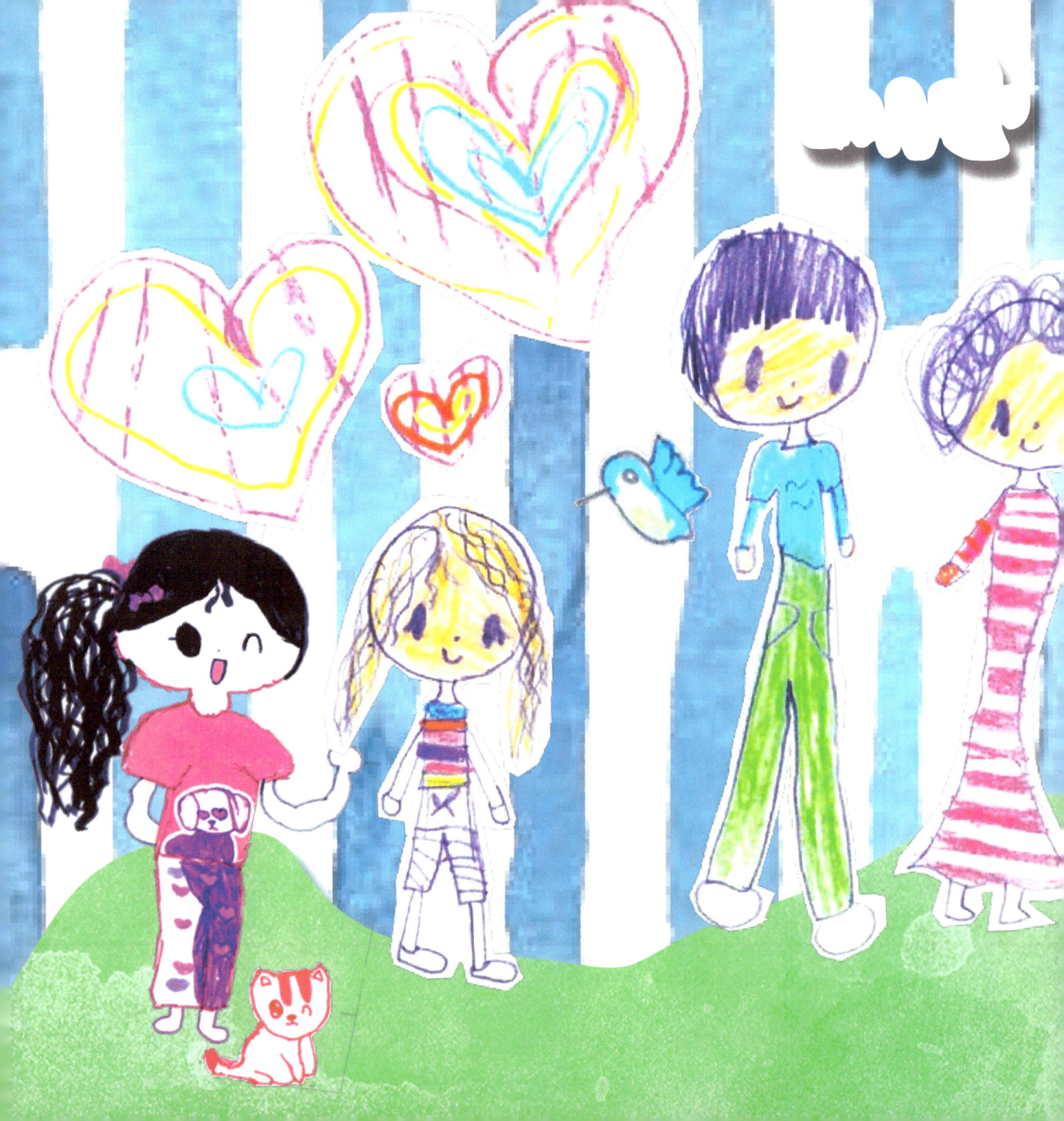

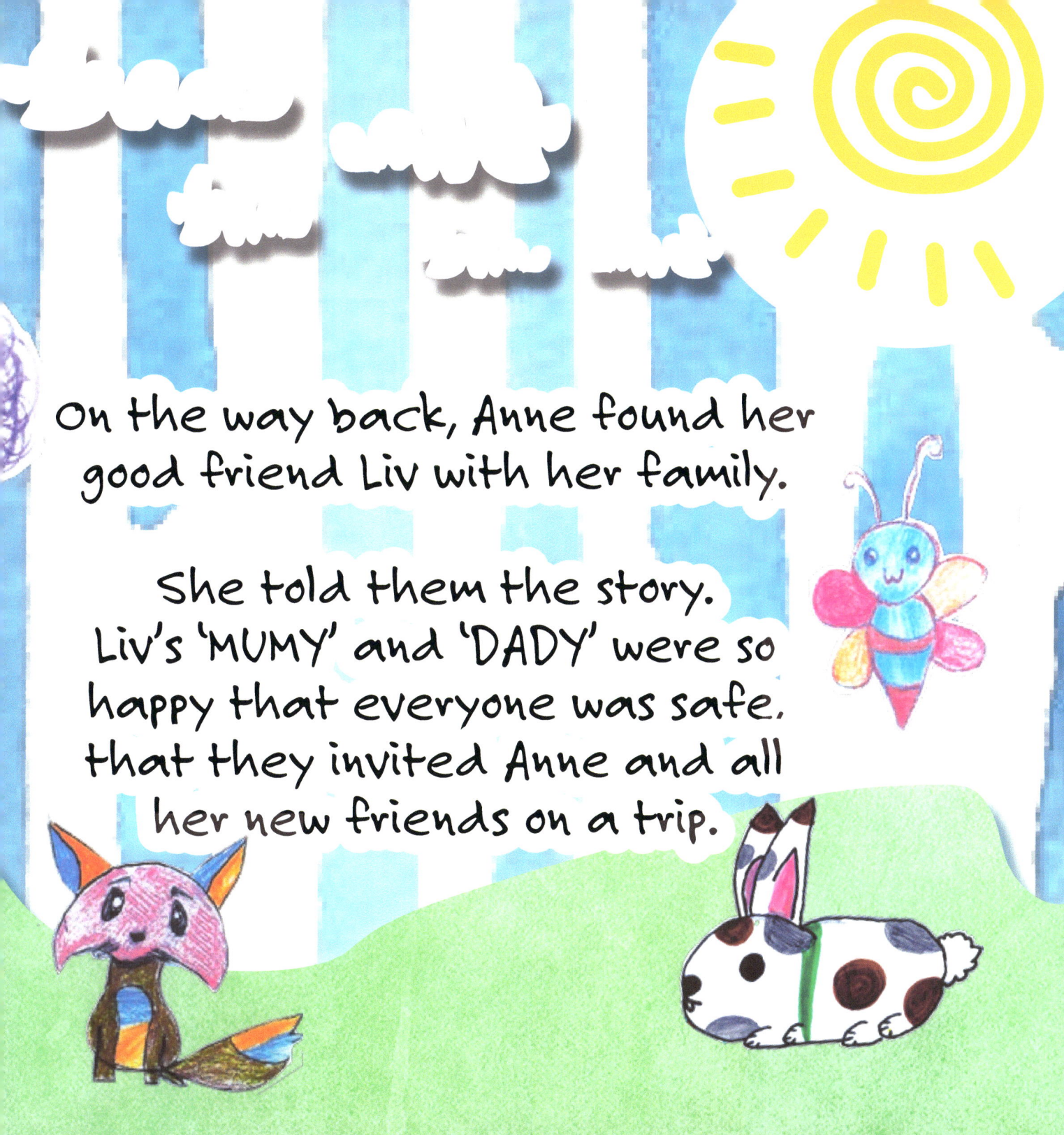

On the way back, Anne found her good friend Liv with her family.

She told them the story. Liv's 'MUMY' and 'DADY' were so happy that everyone was safe, that they invited Anne and all her new friends on a trip.

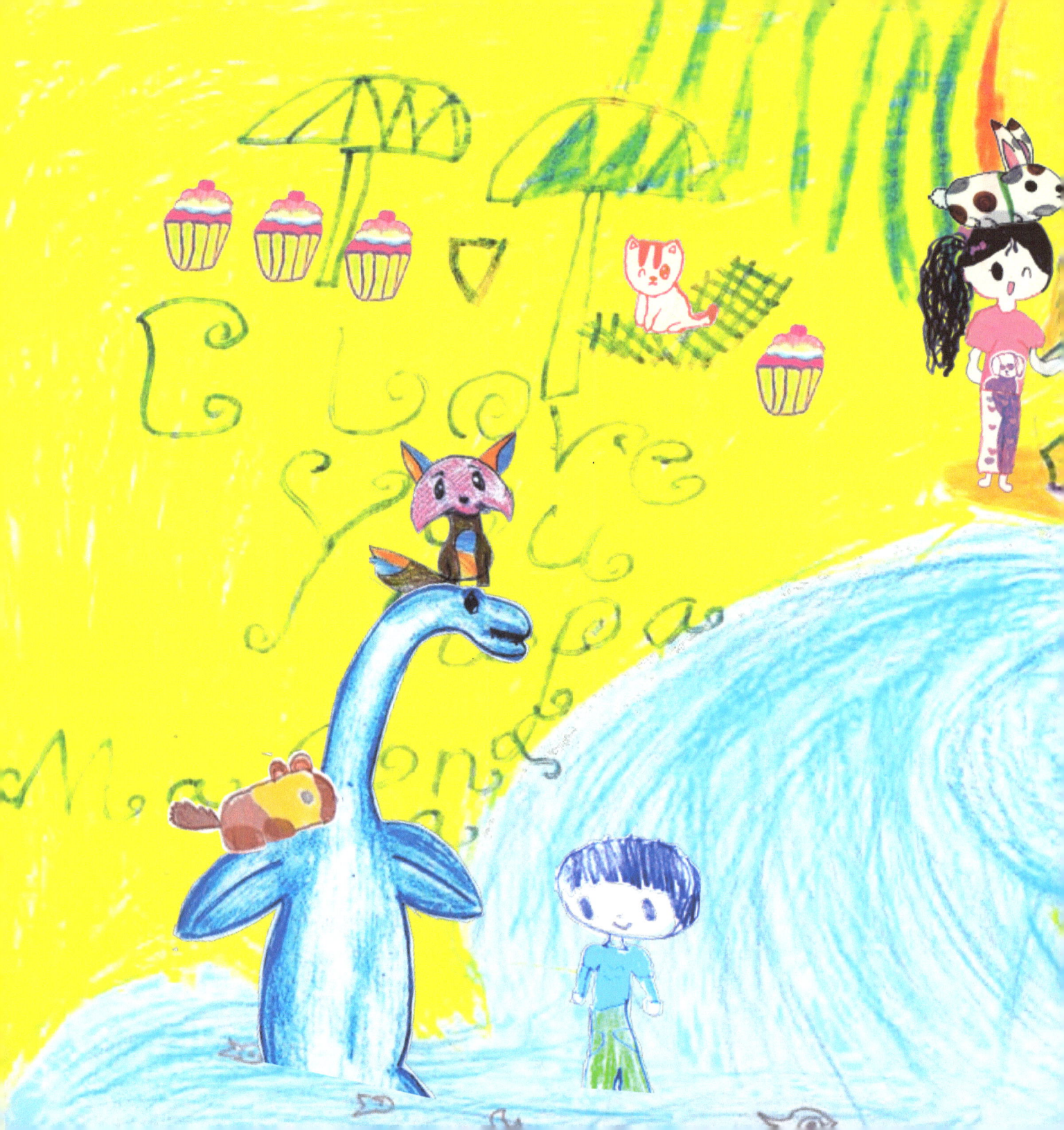

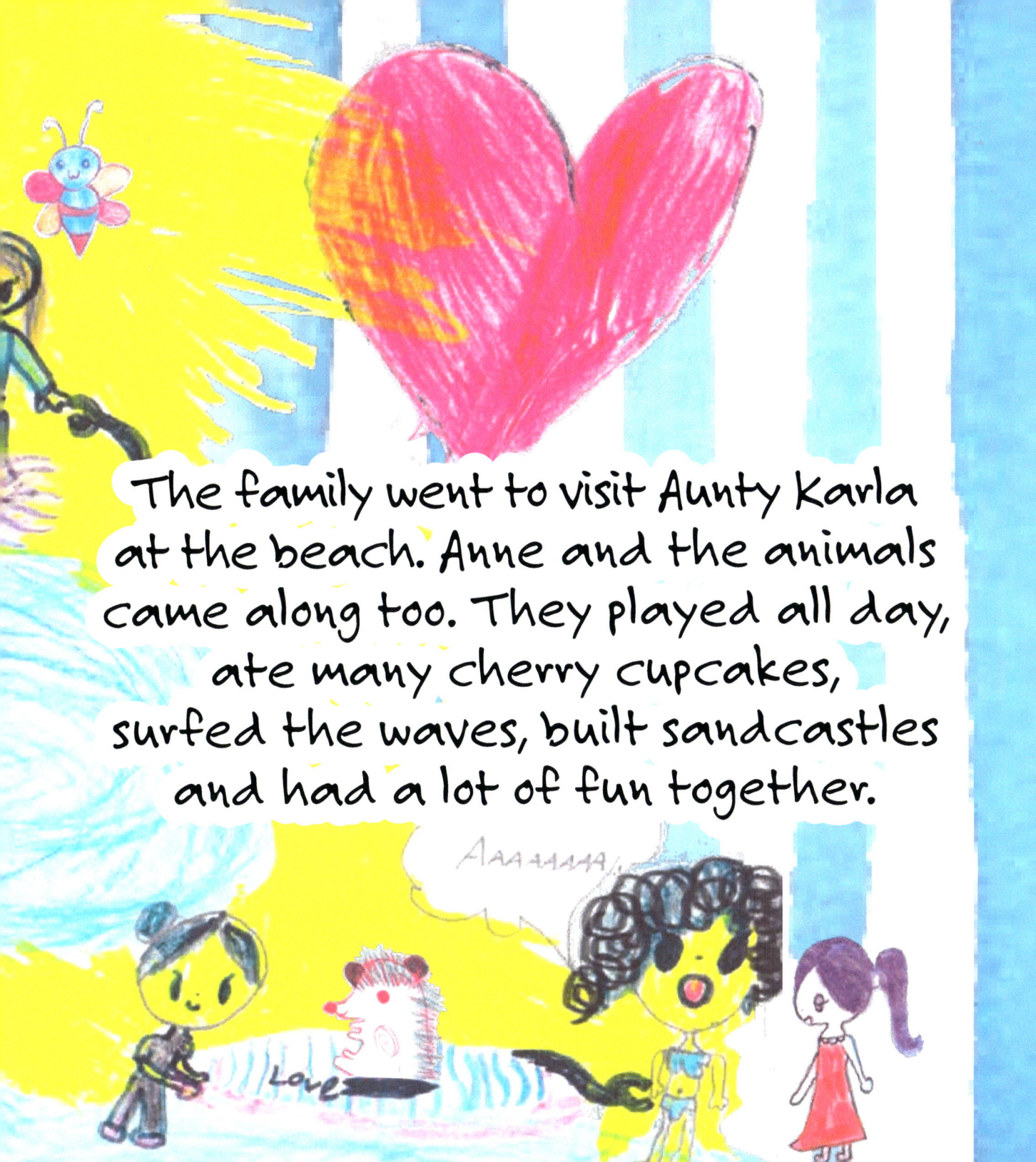

The family went to visit Aunty Karla at the beach. Anne and the animals came along too. They played all day, ate many cherry cupcakes, surfed the waves, built sandcastles and had a lot of fun together.

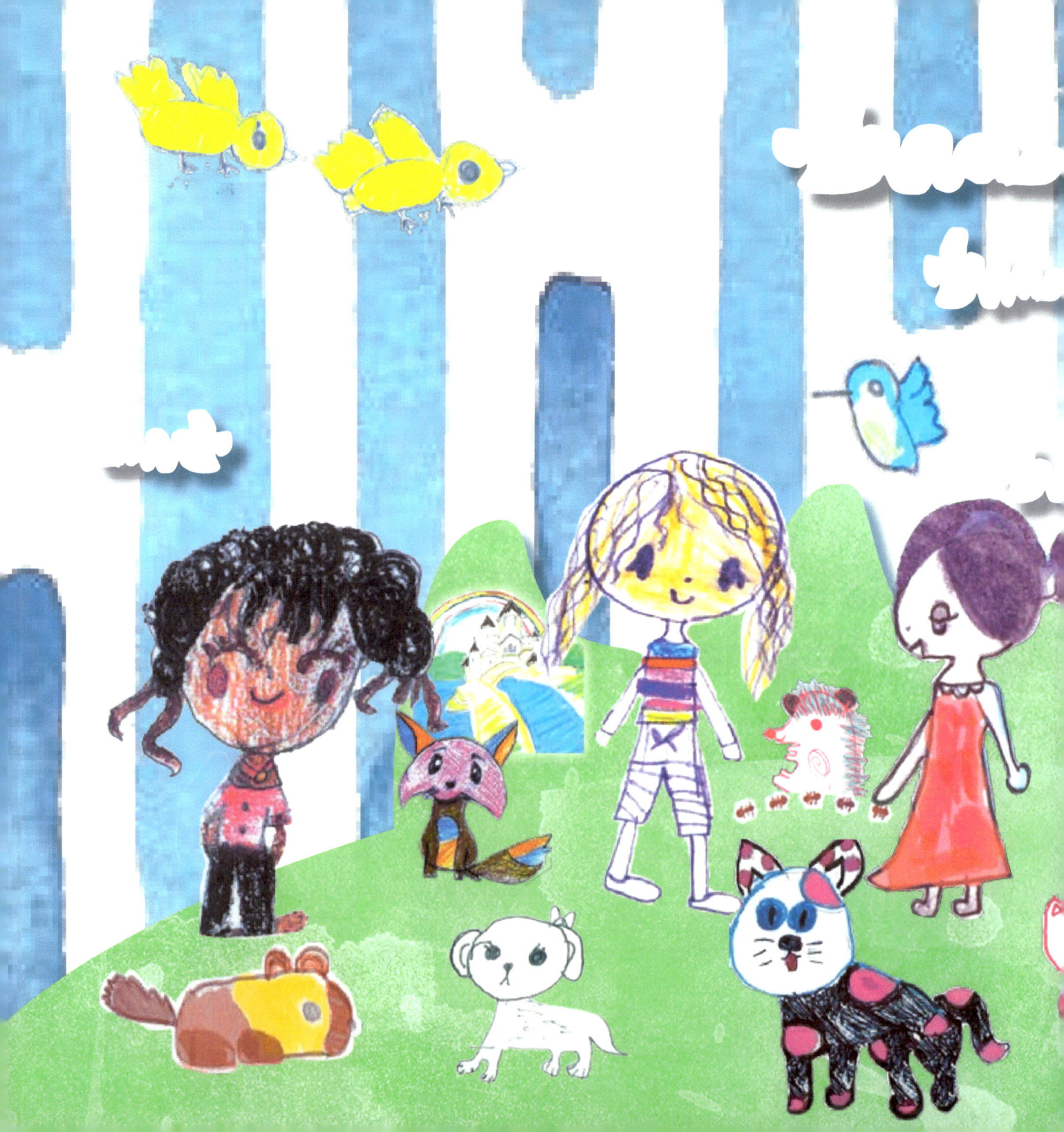

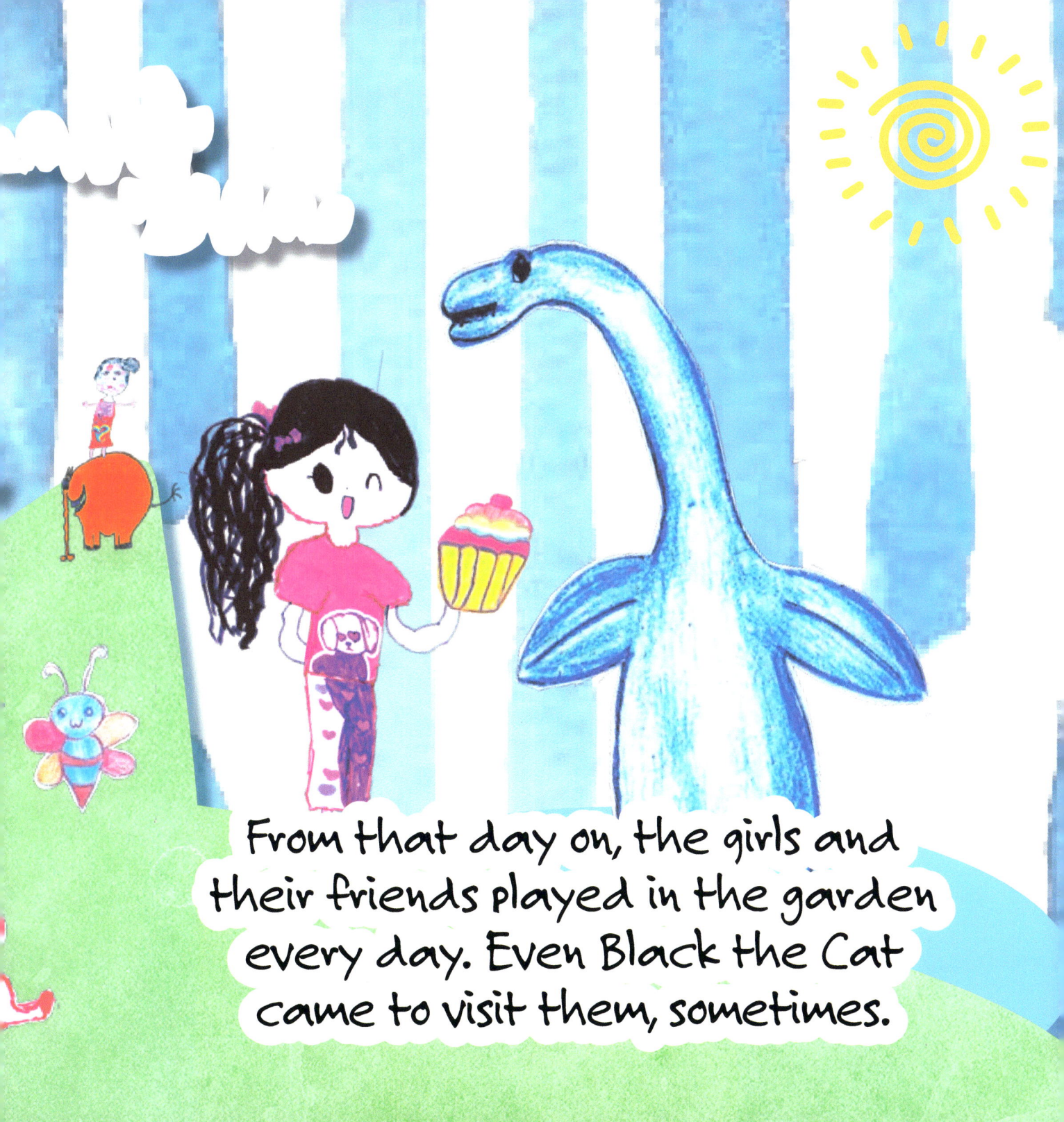

From that day on, the girls and their friends played in the garden every day. Even Black the Cat came to visit them, sometimes.

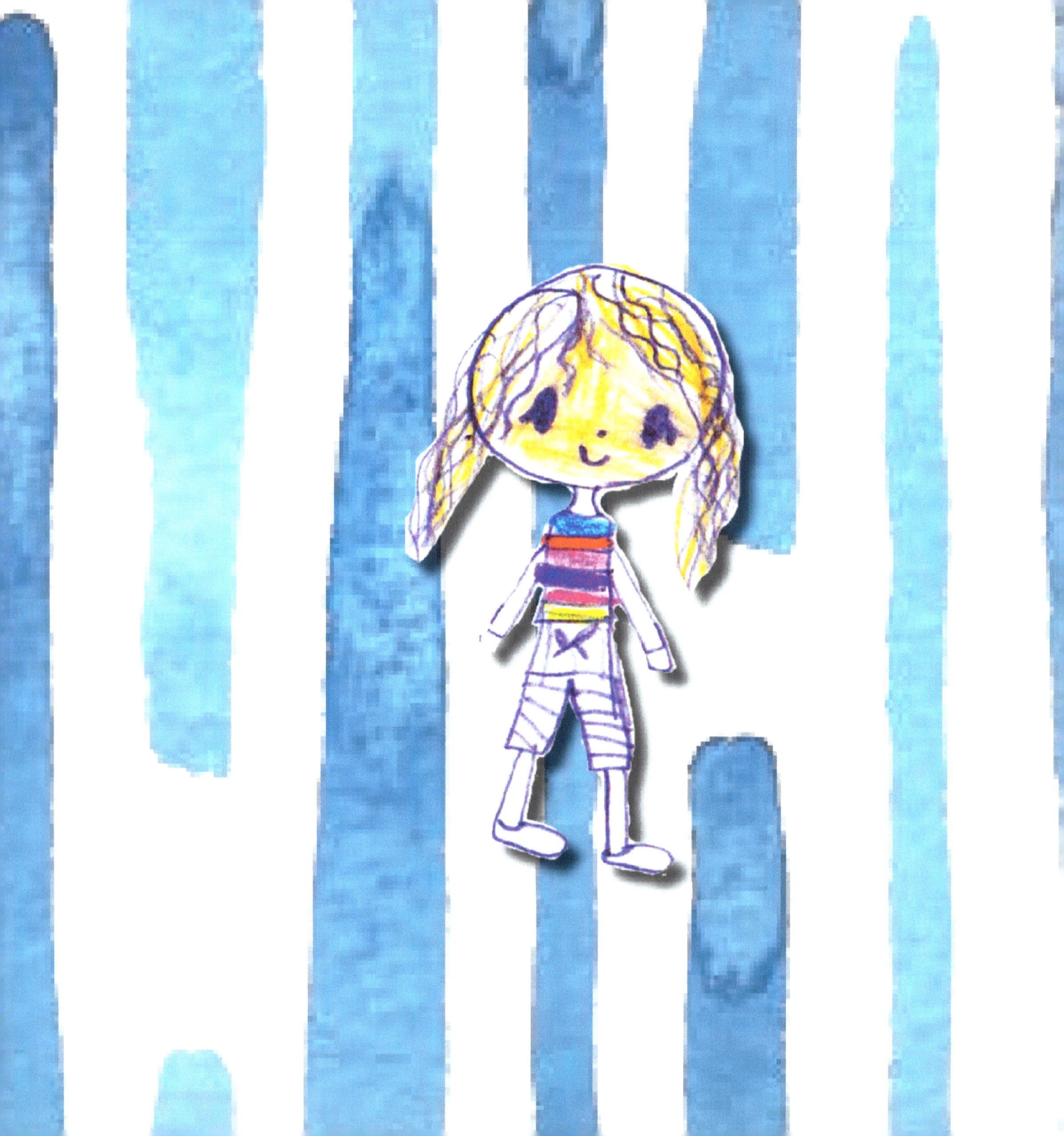

The End

And here are some of my favorite characters to colour

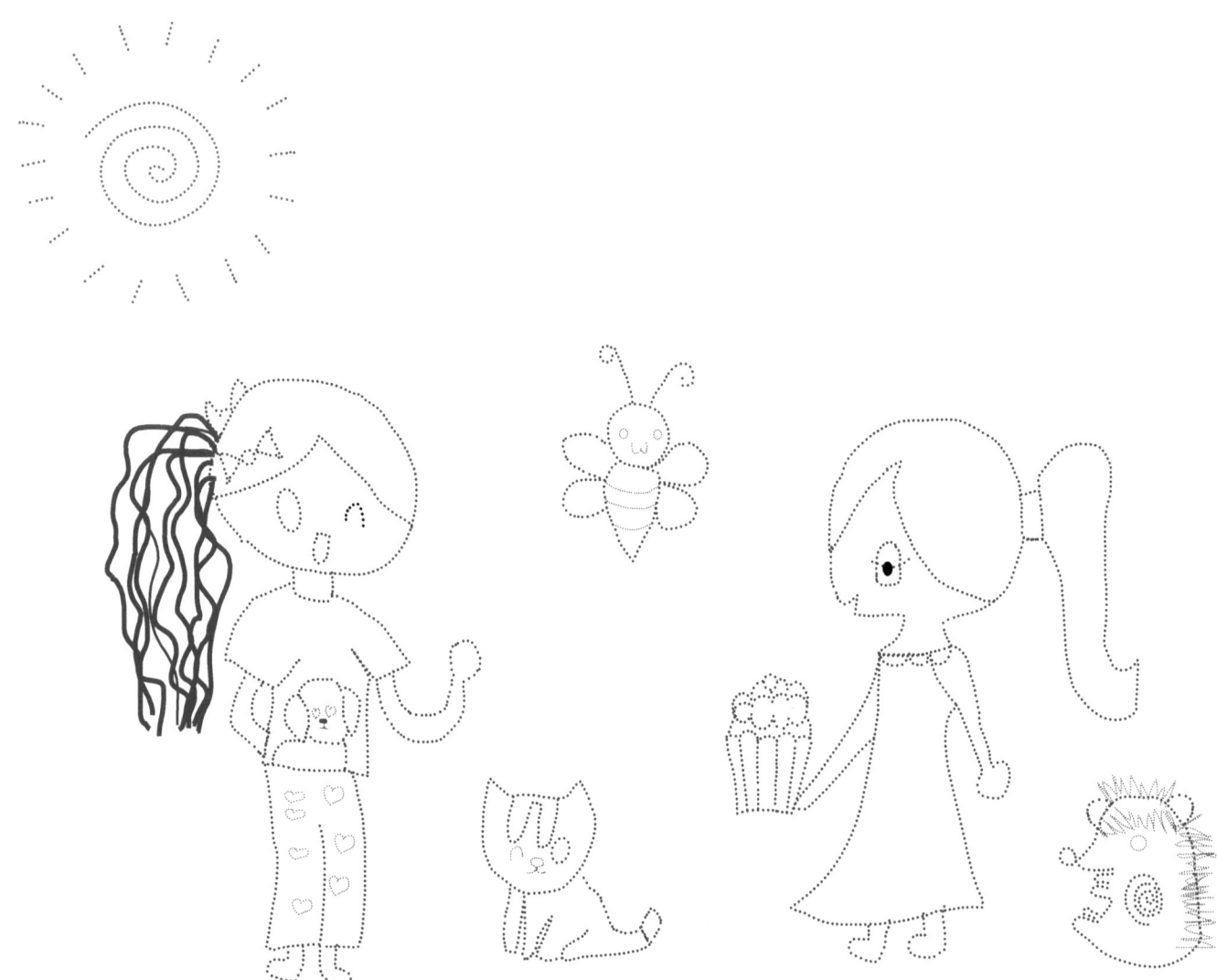

Or you may like to create your own characters for a new story.

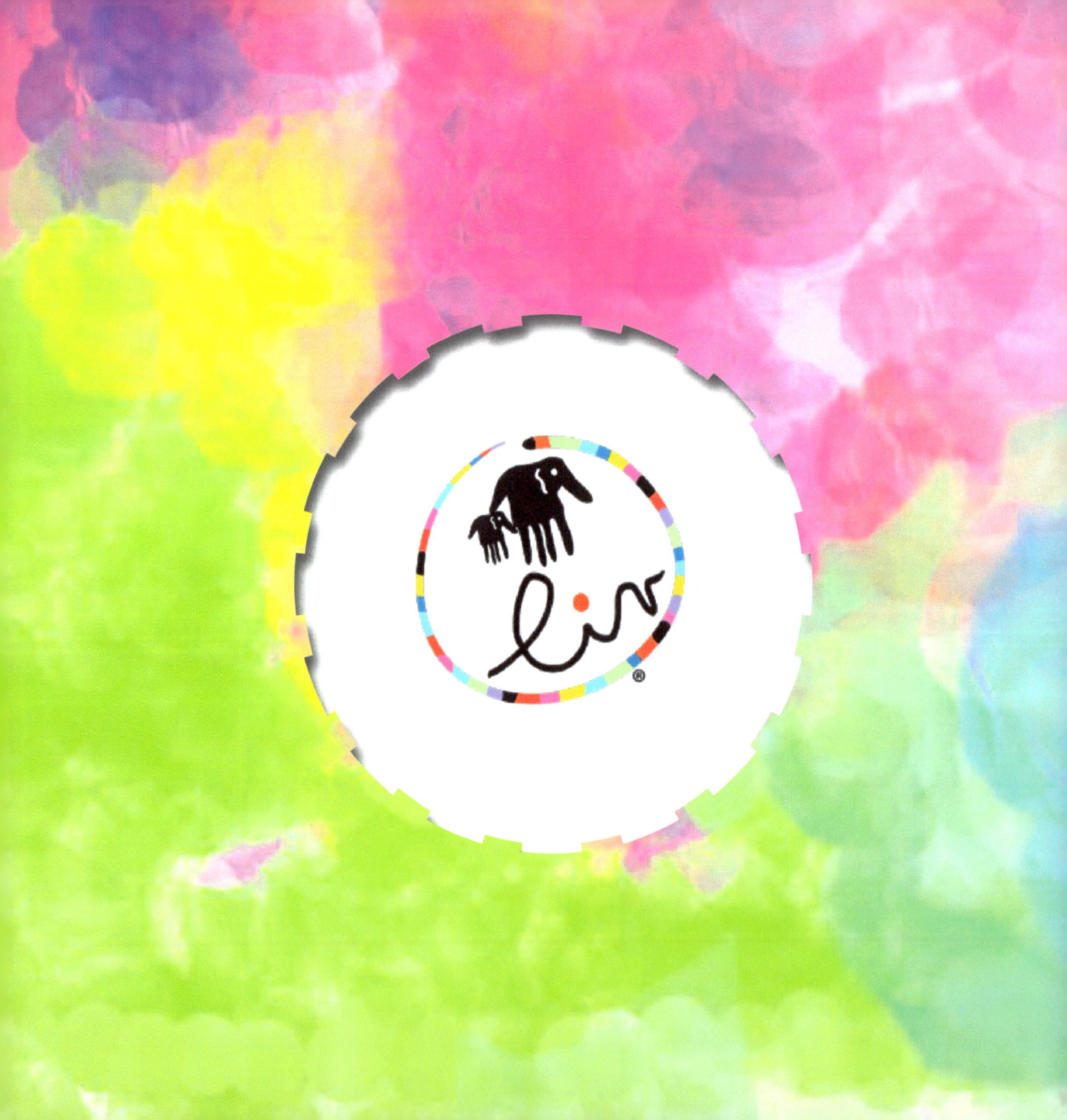

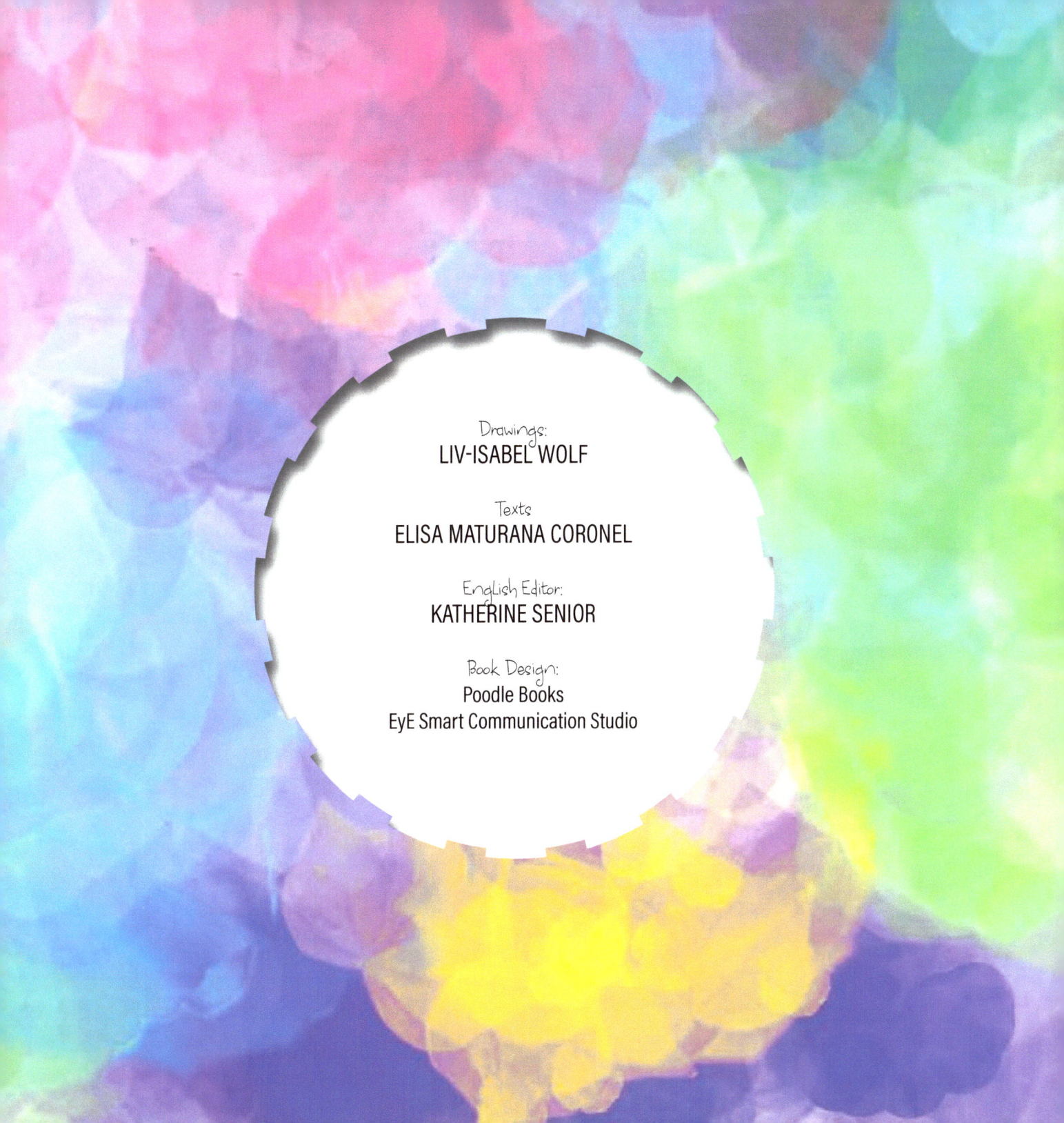

Drawings:
LIV-ISABEL WOLF

Texts
ELISA MATURANA CORONEL

English Editor:
KATHERINE SENIOR

Book Design:
Poodle Books
EyE Smart Communication Studio

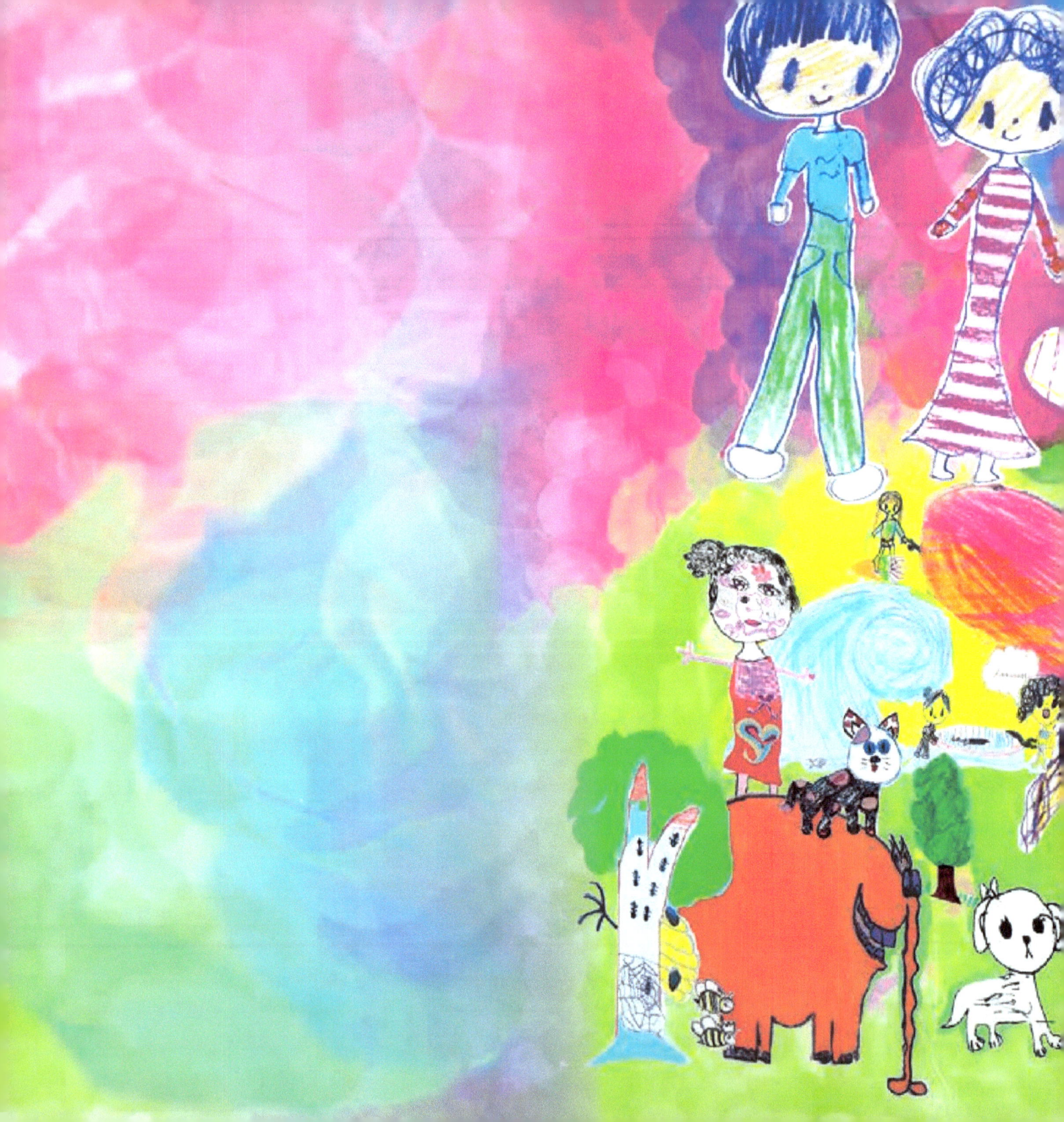

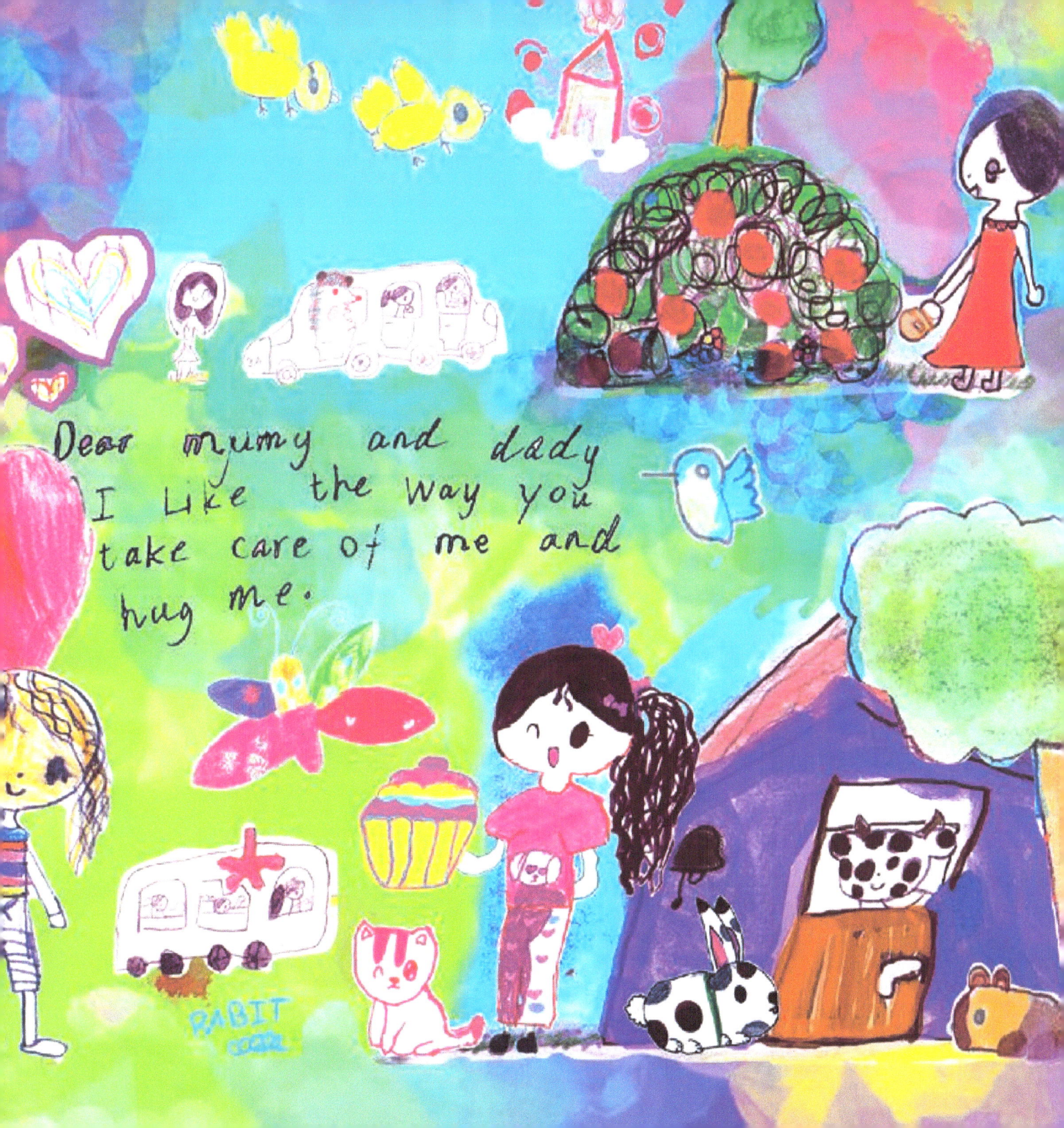

www.ingramcontent.com/pod-product-compliance
Lightning Source LLC
Chambersburg PA
CBHW051219220526
45473CB00003B/1093